# Source Supreme

Advanced Practices for Spiritual Awakening

# Source Supreme

Advanced Practices for Spiritual Awakening

*Ron Kurz, Ellen Laura, Mary Jean Valente*

**Source Supreme**: Advanced Practices for Spiritual Awakening

© 2014 Ron Kurz, Ellen Laura, Mary Jean Valente.

Edited by Helen Emerson

ISBN: 978-0-931689-43-7

**www.TheSourceSupreme.com**

Cover Photo: The Spiritual Hierarchy's presence over the Pacific Ocean, Maui, Hawaii.

Blue Star Photo: The Blue Star, You, Soul, The Inner Master.

**This book is dedicated to The Silent Ones.**

*The Agents of Source Supreme who are responsible only to IT. They are in command of the great Sound Current and give aid and comfort to the Source Supreme. The Silent Ones are also in charge of the mechanical phases of Dense and Subtle Realms and Universes.*

**Please read the entire book first for an overview.**

Then go back and begin your study. Read and re-read each sentence slowly. See each word being imprinted upon the page as you read as though it was issuing forth from you. Ponder upon each word, word combination and sentence. Do not read on if you do not understand a word or a sentence. Ask to be shown and comprehend the true meaning. Fulfill your own destiny and Self-Mastery. Please do not write to us asking questions, as that will defeat the purpose of the information given in this book and hold you back from your own Self-Mastery. Go direct as an individual acquiring freedom on all levels of life.

# TABLE OF CONTENTS

# FOREWARD

## *Personal Responsibility*

**Disclaimer:** The information contained in this book has been compiled and given to us by many wise advanced Spiritual Beings over many lifetimes. We have found it to be the Truth for ourselves and it is expressed as our *personal opinions and worldview guaranteed under the First Amendment of the Constitution of The United Sates of America.*

We offer it to you with the highest intention for your spiritual evolution and for the good of all Beings in all worlds.

The Authors and Copyright Holders have no affiliation with, nor do they endorse any religious, spiritual or metaphysical organization. The information in this book is presented and written in their own words and in universal terminology. If any content may appear to be similar in nature to other writings, it is purely coincidental. Words, sentences, and word phrases that may be used have been stated in various languages throughout time and cannot be copyrighted: Example; God, Spirit, Inner Master, Divine Love, etc.

The reader and/or practitioner of the Self-Contemplations hereby agrees to Indemnify, Forever Defend and Hold Harmless the Authors and Copyright Holders of this book, including All Affiliates, Employees, and their respective Families, or anyone acting on their behalf from any and all such claims, expenses, damages, harm, self-induced trauma or destruction suffered physically, emotionally and mentally which may result from the reader's misinterpretation of the information contained in this book.

*You read and practice the content and Self-Contemplations under your own volition.* There are no secrets in life. All is revealed when you make the conscious effort to *know* Truth. Religious and metaphysical groups have a purpose as you search for higher understandings, however no one but YOU can raise your awareness to the Gems of Truth that already exist within YOU and the HEAVENLY REALMS. Do not be duped or fooled by false teachers or so-called, self-proclaimed spiritual masters. Test and challenge every thing and every one by going to your Inner Temple.

The information contained in this book is presented in Divine Love and should not be misinterpreted to be an attack upon any individual, ethnic race, religion, organization, nation or the United States Government. The Authors and Copyright holders fully support The United States Government as set forth by the U.S. Constitution.

## *Chapter Overviews*

This book is about *Spiritual Awakening to the Source Supreme.* What is essential is for you to evolve and upgrade three areas of your life: 1) Discernment, 2) Discipline, and 3) Divine Love for All Life. The Self-Contemplations included here are essential to make this real to you and move beyond theory. *When you awaken your connection to Source Supreme your physical life also becomes invigorated and enlivened.*

Now is the time to sincerely make the commitment to let go of unnecessary religious beliefs, self-help groups and outdated organizations. It is time to evolve and demand a higher Truth and let go of lies, deception, conditioning and propaganda.

This is an invitation to your deeper awakening and a powerful connection to Source Supreme. Each individual is so unique and there are thousands of variations of consciousness. That is why you must not accept a homogenized version of spiritual practices. Some of you move along rapidly for a while, and then plateau. Some move forward steadily. As soon as someone tells you what pace to move at or how to advance, put your invisible protective shields up for a moment. Remember, you are unique and the journey must be customized for you; sometimes rapid, sometimes slow, so to keep your physical and inner life balanced.

What is essential is that you continue to evaluate your habits; both the positive habits that move you forward and the fear-based, negative habits that hold you back. Look at these habits and conditioned responses with eyes wide-open. We will cover this more in depth in later chapters.

Saints, mystics and sages have written about the Divine Universal Principles for eons. What we offer here is for you, living in the 21st century. As you read, you will recognize the Truth that resonates with your highest spiritual Self.

This Physical world, with its beauty and suffering, is one of a myriad of worlds with duality. Within this duality, 99.9% of everyone here, everyone you know, is here, not by choice, but because of the lies, deception and control of the Gods and Goddesses, prophets and preachers, both ancient and newly self-proclaimed.

The system of religion and karma set forth by these false ones is designed to confuse and keep you involved in seeking comfort instead of freedom and bouncing around between accepting and rejecting your true Self and detesting your neighbors, both close by and around the world.

Many of you, in your sincere attempt to become spiritual, sing praise to these enslavers. Some of you are realizing it's time to stop this and take another journey. The lies and deceptions are so cunning and prevalent everywhere today, with rampant propaganda causing self-induced, self-perpetuating delusions.

Even if you do know this, you may still feel nervous, anxious or embarrassed when you uncover the lies. This nervousness and anxiety come from having accepted answers from the deceivers and a need to "save face." That's why many accept unhealthy or seemingly benign distractions or embrace religious zealotry. Beware; these falsehoods are designed to keep you asleep.

In the 1960s' a man brought forth to the Western world, the truth of how to become Spiritually free. Because only a few were interested enough to hold to these truths on how to live in these Realms and remain free and protected, more lies and propaganda have come forth in the past 50 years. Today it's up to you to protect and guard your mind and your emotions from the propaganda.

*There may be a way out for you.* A way for you to reclaim your Omnipotence, Omniscience and Omnipresence. If these three words mean anything to you, then you are most blessed.

The journey begins with considering Seven Awakenings. Each Awakening can also be considered an initiation into a higher consciousness.

Indwelling within this Physical Realm there is the essence of the Source Supreme. For many of you it is so obvious you are in touch with it moment to moment. For some, the negative forces have gained dominance of your mind and emotions. That is because this Physical

World is a warring universe of positive and negative forces controlled by negative Beings and energies. How is this possible when there is so much beauty and tenderness here? You must be open to seeing the total Truth, and then the answer becomes obvious.

Yes, the Physical world is a Realm of very coarse vibrations. However, it is not too late to declare yourself in alliance with the Source Supreme of Divine Love.

## The Kali-Yuga

For those that know, this is the age of the Kali Yuga, also known as the Iron Age, in which this world has gone berserk with defective thinking and negativity. So much of the mental unrest is due to the unseen forces of the Kali Yuga, including the astrological influences and psychic negativity.

Various religions have written about this cycle of time and the decline in spiritual values. There is always some hot-spot violence raging somewhere on this planet. The decline in consciousness can be seen in much of the music, movies, books and television shows with a strong focus on death, destruction and strange psychic phenomena.

There are escalating reports worldwide of widespread poverty, war, disease, addictions, physical disasters, human sex trafficking, along with abuse of children and animals. In many countries, including the

USA, jails are overflowing. Mental confusion has taken hold to the point where people don't know what to do about these conditions; therefore, apathy or ineffectual efforts are the norm.

The individual Self, Soul, has become immersed and fascinated with the illusions of the outer world. Most Souls have become lazy and have let the mind and other outside influences take control. Every day some one, some thing or some group is attempting to persuade and control your life. If you have been fortunate enough to rise above this negativity, you are already living as a vehicle for Divine Love.

Renouncing your material life is not the answer, living a balanced life, without grasping and clinging is essential. A wise teacher once said, "You can never become sick enough or poor enough to help anyone." This means that neglecting your physical life or giving up all of your possessions does not uplift or benefit those who are suffering. The best thing you can do for the suffering of the world is awaken to Your True Self and attain optimal health of body, mind and Soul – free yourself from addictions and negativity – as you reach out to help others.

*In this Kali-Yuga, the use of recreational drugs, psychedelics, marijuana, alcohol and, tobacco have kept most people in the Astral and Mental worlds. In order to align with the higher frequencies of the Heavenly Realms, it is recommended that no intoxicants be used while practicing the Self-Contemplations offered in this book.*

## *Propaganda*

Propaganda *is* the most dangerous tool used by ruthless people and negative psychic entities to control you. It is an instrument for dissemination of falsehood, hatred and terror, and one of the wicked plagues of Mankind. Propaganda perpetuates *fear,* which perpetuates control: Create a problem, you react, and these unscrupulous Beings already have a solution to solve the problem to control you. This cycle is known as Problem, Reaction, Solution. It has been used upon an unsuspecting population for centuries.

When an agenda meant to control is met with rejection, in order to manipulate the masses into submission, some event or catastrophic situation is implemented. Necessarily, a solution is offered. This solution is one that you would normally immediately reject. However, once exposed to an event intended to fill you with and keep you in fear and dread, this solution becomes one many people not only accept, but ask for, willingly comply to, defend fiercely and come to believe is for their own good and the good of all. The result is like mass hypnosis but in reality is a fraud based on deceit and negative intention causing compliance on a grand scale and overriding the free will we would normally exercise.

The most cunning propaganda has some kernel of truth and is sugar coated with promises of all good things.

Propaganda distracts you from concentrating on your own internal problems, and causes you to deviate from your true goal of progress and advancement on all levels. It sows seeds of discord, fear, suspicion and despair. It demoralizes you and paralyzes your will and courage creating uncertainty, confusion and chaos.

## Freedom from Fear

*Fear* is a negative emotional response to the perception that you cannot control the outcome of an anticipated situation. Fear is a dark cloak of negativity obscuring your true nature. Some people try to avoid fear by simply remaining unaware and hide in denial. However, burying your head in the sand is a sure way to get yourself into big trouble on all levels of your life.

When the attention returns over and over again to past errors, hurts, and disappointments, you remain anchored to the causes and conditions of these missteps and fear remains an enemy.

*Fear* must never control your life. Fear can help you avoid acting foolishly or keep you stuck inside of limiting conditions. *Fear is a frequency of alertness and when you engage your discernment, discipline and Divine Love, you can see the Truth behind each fear and you can then shatter it so it loses its grip on you.* Freedom from fear is the peak of spiritual attainment.

The majority of Humankind lives in the coarse density of the outer world. The true definition of a materialist is: one who relies entirely on the five physical senses to move through life. Some of you have found the *worlds within,* and it is the inner worlds that make the outer world. The world within is One with the Universal Source Supreme, the world in which "we live and move and have our being," the great creative principle of the universe.

The world within is creative. Everything you find on the outside has been created from the Realms within, created by you and your agreement with the Spiritual Hierarchy and the collective consciousness of the time.

As a creative Being, the spiritual power and energy you access depends largely on your attitude and attention and meeting with the True Spiritual Friend. Throughout history there have always been those who align with Source Supreme, sometimes referred to as Spiritual Masters or True Spiritual Teachers. The great saint and poet, Rumi, referred to his Spiritual Master as the "True Spiritual Friend." The attitude of considering the Spiritual Master as your True Friend is the correct attitude.

We emphasize throughout this book that in this time period it is rare to find an authentic Spiritual Teacher so we do not advocate that you seek a physical teacher. This will be expanded upon in future chapters.

By engaging your discernment, discipline and Divine Love you gain the correct attitude to advance spiritually. To begin, focus on *forgiveness and revision* to free your attention so it can dwell completely upon Divine Spirit and illuminate your consciousness.

## Revision As a Daily Practice

You can revise each day to align with Divine Spirit, and by experiencing your revised speech and actions, not only do you modify the trend of your life story but turn all its discords into harmonies. Relive your day as you wish you had lived it, revising the scenes to match your positive ideals.

*The benefit of forgiving is as much for yourself as for the person you are forgiving.*

If forgiveness does not come easily, find a place of compassion and understanding. Compassion is that quality, which instills softness in our hearts for those who may have caused us to be angry or feel wronged. When we can find a thread of compassion we can more easily find the path to forgiveness. Look for that which the situation is teaching you, what you may have contributed to the situation and where, in your own consciousness, you can expand and open to be a greater vehicle for Divine Love.

To further elevate this practice, once you find forgiveness and compassion, consider embracing

Humility and expressing Gratitude. Give thanks to that person and the lesson you have learned that has changed and expanded your consciousness and your vibration transforming you to an even higher state of expression of Source Supreme.

Once you discover the secret of revision you cannot do otherwise than let Divine Love guide you. Your effectiveness will increase with practice. Forgiveness and revision will become one in the same.

Every evening when you go to bed do a mental review of the day. This is an ideal time to practice revision. Is there anyone you need to forgive? Talk to them. Is there anyone that needs to forgive you? It is important to cleanse your consciousness nightly so that resentment will not accumulate.

To change your life you must do more than just forgive, you must change your inner speech. Inner speech reveals the state of consciousness from which you view the world.

## Self-Contemplation on Forgiveness

It is most important that we free ourselves of guilt, regrets and fear through total forgiveness of others and ourselves before we can enter the Inner Realms and regain our true purpose.

Go to a room where you will not be disturbed and sit in a comfortable chair. Close your eyes and begin to think about the people in your life, past and present, that have done you an injustice. In your spiritual or mind's eye imagine them sitting face to face with you. See their faces as clearly as you can. Look them directly in the eye and speak with them. Tell them that you forgive their prior actions against you. Tell them that you forgive them. Really mean it. See them acknowledging and accepting your heart-felt message of sincerity. Send them Divine Love and feel their burden being lifted. This may take some time and if you feel exhausted you may stop and begin this self-examination again tomorrow.

Once this portion of forgiveness is completed, the next day or week, go to your quiet room, close your eyes and now visualize the various people that you have wronged in your life. Really think about it. Dig deep into your past and locate these people in your mind. See each one, sit with them face to face, look them in the eye and ask them to forgive you. Once again see them accepting your sincere message as they pardon you. Feel the guilt and burdens being lifted from you as each person forgives you.

Roll all this negative energy into a ball with your spiritual hands and imagine a warm golden river flowing away from you. Toss this ball of negative energy into the golden river and watch it flow away from you and melt into this river. Take a very deep breath and feel lightness and spaciousness surround you because you have been forgiven.

## Summary

*Knowledge is never concealed from you or the masses, but most people refuse to see, note and understand the knowledge that is right before them. Most get caught up in emotionalism, swept into tidal waves of Astral impulses under the guise of "good versus evil" and end up with someone else's considerations and not their own. It is time to stop running toward transitory pleasure and hiding from pain and claim the high ground where true joy and peace reside.*

Spiritual Awakening includes Seven Gems of Truth that are united to form a prism of luminous light to guide and protect you and open your consciousness to the Divine Sound Current. A golden thread so strong that it unites each in Divine Love holds these truths together.

These Seven Gems of Truth have been written about as seven universal principles of consciousness of the Source Supreme. For those reading today, each chapter is presented so you will discover treasures that are of the Spirit and shine forth into this world and all worlds.

# CHAPTER 1

## AWAKENING 1: THE ONE SOURCE

The Source Supreme is a magnificent Atom Structure and is the penetrating and all pervading power from which all life springs. IT is Omnipotent, Omniscient and Omnipresent. ITS voice is the Living WORD and ITS body is the Light of the worlds.

The Source Supreme will appear to you or anyone, without the need of any intermediary, provided the individual is endowed with the state of consciousness through which it can manifest. This Spiritual Presence has been expressed through various spiritual teachings throughout history without prejudice.

The greatest saints and Spiritual Masters are consumed with a single pointed love and devotion to the Source Supreme, often inspiring their students and humanity to live a virtuous life.

Whenever you or anyone has brought forth the full expression of Omnipotence, Omniscience and Omnipresence, the Source Supreme becomes known in all worlds in an explosion of Light and Sound. Not everyone becomes conscious of this full expression of the Source Supreme energy at the same moment; however, the Spiritual Presence still penetrates each Being, even in the deepest sleep.

The Source Supreme can be seen as Light with the spiritual eye and heard as Sound with the spiritual ear. The Light is the reflection of the universal atoms, and the Sound is the movement of the atoms in space.

IT aligns ITS full power and magnificence through those who most closely align with ITS true nature. ITS true nature has three virtues: Freedom, Wisdom and Power. These three virtues are expressed in all worlds through a great outpouring of Divine Love.

The Light is Luminous and the Sound is Blissfully Melodious and changes frequency throughout each of the Outer and Inner Worlds. As the power from the Source Supreme flows forth into all worlds and penetrates each of us, IT is calling to us, inviting us to become vehicles to express ITS magnificence.

The most important question to pose to yourself each day is this: Am I accepting the invitation from the Source Supreme to express the three virtues and pour forth Divine Love?

Your responsibility is to understand and unite with these three virtues so you can express them according to your individuality. The solution to every problem we have comes through our opening to the higher consciousness. Others can strengthen and encourage us, but it is our own consciousness that receives the gifts of the Source Supreme, and up to us to be responsible for our thoughts, words and actions. If we are mired down with problems, then the lies and propaganda of the negative forces have gained control.

The Source Supreme emanates a flow of life sustaining energy that is entirely positive, creative and constructive. Each of us then distributes this energy according to our integrity and unique qualities. It takes tremendous discipline to turn away from the lies and propaganda circulating in this Kali Yuga.

It is not wise to "just do whatever floats your boat" or brings temporary happiness. Sometimes a sincere person will say, "I just want to be accepted for myself." Often the person making this appeal is identifying with emotions and thoughts that have been influenced by propaganda. If you do this, you may then be a distributing agent for the negative force – not for Source Supreme. This false identification is the root of all suffering.

From the beginning of time, the various cultures and civilizations on planet earth have described this life giving force of the Source Supreme by many different names. The Christian Bible refers to ITS essence as the "Word." "In the beginning was the Word, the Word was with God, and the Word was God," states the Gospel from St. John. The Eastern teachings and philosophies call it, the Shabda, the Bani. In the western hemisphere, it is more commonly known as, the Audible Life Stream, the Cosmic Current, the Sound Current, the HU, or simply, Spirit.

All that you are and all that you possess are based upon the conscious awareness of IT. You are the microcosm of the macrocosm. By aligning your Self with IT in the invisible worlds within, you create harmony. The result will be harmony in your outer world. Harmony in our world within means our thoughts are directed and guided by Divine Spirit, and we are able to determine for ourselves how any experience will affect us. This harmony results in optimism and affluence, for luminosity and radiance within result in affluence and enthusiasm without.

If you have heard this before and sincerely believe you have lived a life of goodness, yet harmony, optimism and affluence are evasive, what does this mean?

While dwelling in the human state of consciousness, which is the shadow of ultimate reality, none are completely free. Living here in this Physical world, everyone, including you, is subject to the laws of time, space and energy, the laws of matter, economics, race, religion and nationality. This is an agreement with the Realm of the senses we have made in the Human state of consciousness. Once we have renounced this and have accepted the true promise of the Source Supreme, via our mastership within, the Inner Master, which is the *real* YOU, the transition from Human self to the Spiritual Self begins to take place.

This means unplugging all your beliefs and all your energy centers, known as chakras, from the social conditioning of the day. It even means unplugging excessive emotional sympathy for world conditions and replacing that sympathy with compassionate action and Divine Love.

All living Beings, from Humans to animals, although the bodies are transitory, are precious to Source Supreme and meant to be respected, not exploited.

Before you begin to practice visualization, spiritual exercises or Self-Contemplations to achieve greater freedom, do an inventory of your daily actions, thoughts and words. Because this world is mathematical, each moment of each hour is adding either a positive, negative or neutral charge to your life. Do not become neurotic or guilt ridden about the negativity; do your best to view it "charge neutral" and be honest with yourself.

Ask yourself: Do you sing mantras or pray or practice other spiritual activities for an hour or two a day, yet still allow your mind and mouth to be a garbage dump? Do you project anger or Divine love when driving a car through traffic or resolving a challenging problem? Do you smile to someone's face and make belittling comments behind the back?

Do you say things to elevate yourself by putting others down? If you find yourself talking about the negative hurts and errors of the past with a constant need to explain these to other people, you are trapped in the lower emotional Realms.

This does not mean you cannot have a heart to heart talk with a loved one or business associate to improve communication or resolve conflicts. It means that you always ask yourself before you speak: *Is it true, is it necessary, is it kind?*

Destructive thoughts and actions come from negative propaganda and are not natural to us. They can be eliminated through discernment, discipline and Divine Love. Each moment is a new opportunity to bless all Beings and start anew without criticizing anyone or yourself about the past.

We have found it is definitely possible to be free from negative influences and be a vehicle for Source Supreme. The next essential step is Spiritual Protection. This will assure that you will receive the direct flow of the Source Supreme and be a distributing agent for the Light and Sound, without the need of intermediaries.

## Self-Contemplation on Spiritual Protection

You begin your journey with a Spiritual Protection Technique for fortifying yourself from harm, negative people and unwanted thoughts; to protect your mind and emotions, begin by closing your eyes and sitting still in a quiet room where you will not be disturbed for 5 to 15 minutes.

Imagine a powerful luminous White Light entering the top of your head flowing downward to your Heart and Solar Plexus area, then expanding like the rays of the Sun filling your entire body. Every cell and atom in your body glows with ITS essence. Feel the substance, the power and the warmth. See it flowing out of your hands, feet and entire body. You *become* the pure White Light.

Expand the White Light about 10 feet above, below and all around you in the form of a protective egg shape. Walls, floors and ceilings have no meaning or interference. You are now encased in this egg. Fortify your egg casing with the luminous White Light. Make it very real and powerful to you.

You now have an impenetrable protective Shield against all negativity. Know that nothing can enter and penetrate this Shield of White Light except Divine Love. Know that all negativity bounces off your protective Shield and returns from whence it came. Do this technique every day.

Once you have mastered this technique, you can call upon The Shield of White Light of protection while sitting or standing, anywhere at anytime. It is always your personal responsibility to protect your Self on all levels.

# CHAPTER 2

## UNDERSTANDING THE
## SELF-CONTEMPLATION PROCESS

Before we discuss "Awakening 2: YOU Are The Essence," we must understand *Conscious Awareness* and ask: How do I make true contact with the Source Supreme and Divine Spirit? It is through Self-Contemplation and opening the inner eyes and inner ears through initiation. *The Source Supreme initiates you,* Soul, into more luminous Realms of Light and Sound. As this happens your connection to Divine Spirit is strengthened until you truly live, move and have your Being in the heart of the Source Supreme. Fine tune your virtues to the fullest, develop a 360-degree viewpoint, and do not allow others to run your life.

The Self-Contemplations guide you to move beyond self-knowledge and insight. To ascend the higher states of consciousness, you learn the subtle art of catching and holding the Divine Spirit Power so that it flows through you continually.

Awakened Consciousness *is* the key to life. Your desires are states of consciousness seeking to be expressed through you. Your desires are determined by your conception of your Self. Desires should be of Self-expression, creativity and the realization of God, for the good of the whole. Therefore, when manifested, they uplift your Self as well as everyone you meet, and all the Universes of the Source Supreme.

Because all of recorded history as we know it is part of the Kali Yuga, the age where the Inner Light and Sound are veiled and obscured by darkness, most Souls have forgotten that desires are meant to lead us to the Divine.

Here is a brief understanding: There are three ingredients for your True Self, Soul, the Inner Master to make contact with Divine Spirit; 1-Your Consciousness. 2-Your Desire. 3-Your Receptive Attitude.

To contact the Source Supreme is first a matter of *Attitude* and *Attention.* When love for Source Supreme fills your entire Being to the point where your trust and love for IT are all consuming, then your attention is naturally aligned to Divine Spirit.

No matter what your current life condition or karma, when you return to an attitude of *childlike curiosity,* and you are receptive to Divine Love, you wipe the slate clean and contact with the Divine Source manifests. This is when you are truly initiated and a state of grace is bestowed upon you.

*Since your consciousness consists of everything you hold to be true, all of your conscious and subconscious desires manifest accordingly.* This is why some, even after having heard the above over and over, still struggle while others move steadily onward. It is because the subconscious desires and dominant karmic patterns are in conflict with the current conscious desires. This can be resolved through persistent use of the Self-Contemplations given in this book.

How long does it take for manifestation of a clearly stated desire? *The time it takes for a desire to manifest is directly proportional to the feeling of naturalness held in the consciousness.* The feeling of naturalness lets you know that your conscious and subconscious desires are aligned with guidance from Divine Spirit. You can experiment with being specific about what you desire until you come upon the desire which evokes a feeling of naturalness. A specific desire combined with a feeling of naturalness is most powerful. You will then feel a great sense of aliveness, buoyancy and lightness.

A word of Caution and Responsibility: Do you remember the old adage, "Be careful what you wish for... you may get it." Well let's change that a bit. "Be careful for what you wish for...you *will* get it." That is why we emphasize placing your attention, your energies, your desires, on states of consciousness rather than just on things. Let your feelings guide you. A sense of lightness and well-being accompanies the desires that are aligned with Divine Spirit.

For example, say you wanted more money. Money in itself is not negative or positive. It is simply a means of exchange. However, you must consider all the ways you could possibly obtain the money you're asking for *because both your conscious and subconscious desires are at play here.* For instance the house burns down and you collect on the insurance. Someone close to you suddenly dies and you become the beneficiary in the Will. An automobile accident occurs and the physical body is badly damaged, possibly for the rest of its life, but you receive a large sum of money to cover your grief. Is it worth it?

Always focus your *attention* on the consciousness, the feeling of already being how you want to be, which is connected to Source Supreme. Do not focus your *attention* only on things. Your positive *attitude,* your belief of the wish fulfilled, determines the end result. You simply provide the environment, the positive atmosphere for the Divine energies to work through you. The Divine energies are the Light and Sound Current of the Source Supreme.

As you emerge from subjective Self-Contemplations you will know each time by your changed attitude and your new inner speech that you have conceived your desires and met the Inner Master. The Light, the Sound Current and meeting your True Self, the Inner Master will give you the wisdom, power and freedom to fulfill your desires.

You alone are responsible for what you desire and make manifest. Keep your desires on the Source Supreme and all will be added to your world that will sustain a happy, healthy, loving life. It is a spiritual law that we must first seek the kingdom of God. Christ stated this many times: "Seek ye first the Kingdom of Heaven." His Sermon on the Mount is a classic in laying down the basic spiritual law that says we have to have spiritual realization before all things come to us in a natural way.

## Subjective and Objective Realms

Throughout history esoteric and mystical teachings have guided students to become familiar with the subtle energies emanating from the Inner Realms of the Astral, Causal, Mental, Etheric and the higher frequencies of Soul Realms, sometimes called the Heavenly Realms. The purpose of this is to become spiritually free and partake of the beauty and Divine Love that flows from Source Supreme. (See Chapter 5 for the Chart)

Remember: As Within, So Without, As Above, So Below. These terms reflect the relationship of the Subtle and Dense Realms: Etheric, Mental, Causal, Astral and the Physical World. Anything that transpires or happens in these Subtle Realms has a corresponding effect on the Physical Realm.

These Inner Realms are invisible to the physical eyes and ears, but can be perceived as one develops spiritually through initiation. The Inner Realms have corresponding bodies made of subtle energies. You, as Soul, have an Etheric body, a Mental body, a Causal body, an Astral body and a Physical body.

The Physical Realm is one of emotion and form. Immediately above is the Astral, a Realm of raw emotion and force. Next is the Causal where "seeds" and "records" of all events from this and previous lives are stored. The Mental Dimension is a Realm of endless forms involved with the Mind through thought, volition and analysis. Just above is the Etheric. Its primary function is for your True Self, Soul, to communicate with the subtle bodies that correspond with each realm.

All these Dimensions or Realms are interrelated, so what happens in one has a direct influence on what happens on the others. Keep this in mind when Self-Contemplating your desires. Know that somewhere, in some place in time in the Dense Worlds, your desires, thoughts, emotions, and actions will manifest.

This is why we must consider ourselves in two lights: our relationship to the outer world (the objective reality) and our relationship to the inner world (subjective reality) to live a balanced life and advance spiritually.

The outer Physical Realm is composed primarily of dense matter, which is animated by the energies from the Subtle Inner Realms.

Each body vibrates in a unique way as Soul pours Tuzashottama (Soul energy) to these bodies to keep them healthy and vibrant. This is why we will repeatedly direct you to the Self-Contemplations. *The Tuzashottama energy is powerful, yet it cannot be stored; it lives in the present and must be generated and renewed each day to keep you healthy and open as a positive conduit for Divine Spirit.*

Understanding and accessing this Soul energy brings us to a deeper understanding of human love and Divine Love. Human love is like a candle and generates warmth and light to those close to us. Divine Love is like the sun in the sky, generating warmth and light to the entire planet and all beings. When our Soul energy is activated and flows through our subtle bodies we are better able to give and receive both human and Divine Love.

While living in this Kali Yuga, there are more challenges to keep the subtle bodies open to the positive flow of Divine Love. Just as the Physical body can become weakened, ill or disabled the subtle bodies can also become weakened. When this occurs, the behavior of the individual becomes unhealthy or even dangerous.

There are a myriad of conditions that cause harm to the subtle bodies, such as indulging in anger, hatred, envy and deception, or polluting the body with drugs and alcohol, to name just a few. When the subtle bodies are weakened, they are susceptible to negative influences and propaganda and this is why some individuals are plagued with ongoing problems even after many attempts to improve the outer life through prayer, affirmations, psychotherapy, and a variety of self-improvement programs. This is what is meant when it is said you must heal from the inside because when the subtle bodies heal, you see authentic change in the physical life.

## Receptivity and Imagination

When first learning how to Self-Contemplate, assume a receptive attitude of mind, a listening attitude, and if need be, *imagine* hearing the voice of a great spiritual teacher you have chosen to speak to you and teach you what you desire to know. *Imagine* that you hear the teacher tell you that you have that which you desire to know and to be. You remain in this receptive state until you *feel the thrill* of having heard the good and wonderful news. Then go about your business in secret telling no one of this wonderful inner experience, confident that in due season you will experience this desired outward manifestation. Eventually, you will come to realize that you are in direct communication with the Divine. YOU and the Source Supreme are One.

*Imagination, enthusiasm and faith* are the faculties required to create objective conditions. *Imagination transcends time and space. Recognition of a state vibrates or awakens it via the Sound Current.*

When in Self-Contemplation, stay in the *present moment,* the *Here* and *Now.* Do not visualize your Self at a distant point of space and at a distant point in time. Instead, make elsewhere *here,* and the future, *now.* The future event is a reality *now* in a dimensionally larger universe and *now* in a dimensionally larger universe is equivalent to *here* in the ordinary three-dimensional space of everyday life. The difference between *feeling* your Self in action, *Here* and *Now,* and visualizing your Self in action as though you were on a motion picture screen, is the difference between success and failure of contacting the Source Supreme and Divine Spirit.

Look as though you see, listen as though you hear, stretch forth your hands as though you touch and your assumptions harden into facts. Intense and deep Self-Contemplation brings about union with the state contemplated and during this union we have experiences, lessons and behave in keeping with our change of consciousness. You will discover that every time you retire into your personal Inner Temple, through true Self-Contemplation, your externalization of time and space becomes dimensionally larger. This is proof in itself that the other side of the veil, the Source Supreme exists *Here* and *Now.*

To feel and to know the *presence* of Divine Spirit, to subjectively actualize a state by impressing upon your Self, through a feeling, a definite conscious state *is* the secret of all secrets. Therefore, *assume* the *feeling* that would be yours were you already in possession of your wish and the wish *must* be realized. "As Within, So Without." Have a true loving romance and enchantment with Divine Spirit and the Source Supreme and all things are possible.

## Self-Contemplation on Activating your Physical Sun, the Solar Plexus

We must provide a relaxed atmosphere for the Divine Light and Sound Current to manifest through our Being and be free from tension. Our next step is to relax mentally and "let go" of all adverse conditions, such as hatred, anger, worry, jealousy, envy, sorrow, trouble and disappointment of any kind. These are sometimes referred to as passions of the mind.

Tension leads to mental unrest and abnormal mental activity of the mind. It produces worry, concern, fear and anxiety. *Relaxation must be cultivated and achieved in order to make contact with The Light and Sound Current of Divine Spirit.* Mentally determine that you will relax every muscle and nerve, until you feel quiet and restful and at peace with your Self and the Physical World. The Solar Plexus, your Sun, will then be ready to function and you will be surprised at the results.

Regarding your Solar Plexus, it has been likened to the Sun of the Physical body, because it is a central point of distribution for energy that the Physical body is constantly generating. This energy is distributed from your nerves to all parts of your body. If this radiation is very strong within you it could be said you are filled with personal magnetism. You may become positively radiant and wield an immense power for good. Your presence alone, without a spoken word, will often bring peace, serenity and comfort to troubled minds and people with emotional problems. When your Solar Plexus is in active operation and radiating the life force, people you come in contact with will have pleasant and joyful sensations. However, if there are any interruptions of this radiation, the sensations are unpleasant and the flow of the life force energy to some part of your Physical body is stopped.

Your Solar Plexus is the point at which the parts meet the whole, where the finite becomes infinite, where the uncreated becomes created, the universal becomes individualized, and the invisible becomes the visible. *Your Solar Plexus is located above the stomach and just below the chest or the diaphragm.* It is the point at which life appears, and there is no limit to the amount of life you may generate from your Solar Plexus Center. You can accomplish whatever it is directed to do. It is here that the power of the conscious mind lies. The subconscious can and will carry out your plans and ideas as it is suggested to it by the conscious mind.

All you have to do is let your Light shine! The more energy you can generate, the more quickly you will transmute undesirable conditions into sources of pleasure for the good of all.

Remember, non-resistant thought expands the Solar Plexus; resistant thought contracts it. Pleasant thought expands it, unpleasant contracts it. Thoughts of courage, power, and confidence produce a corresponding state. However, the arch-enemy of the Solar Plexus is *fear* and must be absolutely destroyed before there is any possibility of letting your Light shine. It must be expelled forever. When fear is destroyed your Light will shine forever! When you discover that you are One with the Divine Source Supreme, fear is destroyed and you regain your power, your energy and your life.

Take your normal position in your quiet room, place your attention on your spiritual eye between your eyebrows and begin to *see* and *feel* The White Light of Divine Spirit entering from above down through the top of your head, known as the Crown Chakra. See your Crown Chakra open like the petals of a beautiful rose as the White Light engulfs your head, traveling through your Physical body illuminating your Sun, your Solar Plexus, in the center of your chest. *Know* that this sacred White Light is moving from your Solar Plexus through your entire physical nervous system clearing any blockages you may have that may prevent you from emanating the Divine energy of Source Supreme. With each pulsating ray of this luminous White Light, your Sun now radiates with pure positive clarity.

Remember there is no rush. You can do this Self-Contemplation for a few days or a few weeks until you feel this clearing has been accomplished. Only you can determine when you are ready to move on to other Awakenings.

# CHAPTER 3

## AWAKENING 2: YOU ARE THE ESSENCE

The second awakening is this: You, Soul, are the manifested individualized essence of the Source Supreme. By understanding the first two awakenings all questions about "why am I here, what is my purpose" can be put to rest.

Protect and claim your identity as Soul. Let nothing get in the way of your identity as Soul. Each of us is an individual Being and a cosmic world unto ourselves. Our individual vibrational harmony with the Light and Sound is what makes us unique. The more we attune to the frequency of Divine Love, the more we become a vehicle for Source Supreme to pour ITS love into all Realms.

When you think and reflect on who you are, create a space between yourself as Soul and all other roles. Say to yourself, I AM. If you must add something to this, then add, I AM Omnipotent, Omniscient, and Omnipresent. Visualize a space the distance of 2 or 3 feet in all directions. Make a physical motion with your arms so you can fill this space with radiant light into which only the Source Supreme dwells. Your Omnipotence, Omniscience and Omnipresence come first and precede any responsibilities as a mother, father, teacher, doctor or friend. If this is forgotten, then the true power of Source Supreme remains dormant in you.

The proper calling of Soul is to distribute the positive and survival qualities of the Source Supreme for the betterment of itself and others and to become whole again with the essence of the Source Supreme of All. Once we have grasped the idea of Source Supreme as the great forming power, we seek IT in itself through receptiveness.

As Human Beings, most everyone loves stories of redemption. We feel uplifted when we hear of someone who triumphs over great suffering, and turns away from vengeance to embrace love. This occurs when the Divine Light and Sound from the Source Supreme is transmitted to the subtle bodies as well as the Physical body, bringing true healing and initiation.

Your responsibility is to engage in healthy activities to strengthen your Physical and Subtle bodies and spend time with those who respect your physical and spiritual development. Get out into nature, show reverence for all living Beings, laugh, sing, dance, cook, garden, read, write, paint, draw, sculpt, invent something new and wonderful to benefit the world – there are so many positive ways to enrich your physical life and keep the subtle bodies protected with the spiritual practices offered here.

## The Formless Power

The invisible formless power flows from Source Supreme and is called Divine Spirit. IT fills the very ethers of the world in a fluid state, and is the life giving Sound. The Light is knowledge and the Sound Current gives it vibratory animation. Divine Spirit has no laws, no interest in anything except to obey the will of those who use it. Beyond the Spiritual Realm of the Soul plane, Divine Spirit becomes so sensitive that even a thought from Soul will have immediate effect and it rushes instantly to obey.

Since Divine Spirit is a law unto itself, it has the power of returning to the sender whatever you might be sending to the holy essence of life. Thus, the Spirit of the Source Supreme, in the Physical and Subtle Worlds (Etheric, Mental, Causal, Astral and Physical) works in a dualistic manner. It can curse you the sender, or it can bless you.

Divine Spirit is the greatest spiritual force of all ages. The person who doubts this in the beginning will learn in time that nothing triumphs in life unless it has the element of Divine Spirit in its own nature. By practicing the teachings in this book you, Soul, will be entering into the Self-knowledge or Self-realization state of consciousness and will awaken your true nature.

Life forms, society's laws and civilizations on every planet, and dimension are just what Souls dwelling there have made them. Souls, themselves, as the creative agents of Divine Spirit, have created forms and life everywhere, including space, time, energy and matter. This is the reason that mankind has worshipped gods in ignorance.

The Spiritual Hierarchy is hardly more than a group of Souls working on various levels to keep the world running. They create laws pertaining to the upkeep of their individual planet, or planet worlds and Dimensions, by being distributing agents for Divine Spirit. Some of the Gods/Goddesses of the Spiritual Hierarchy work for the liberation of all, while some demand worship and are perpetuating the propaganda and deception to keep Souls trapped.

*"The Truth about this is very shocking and may be overwhelming to some people who have a strict religious upbringing: God or the Source Supreme is not interested in Human consciousness, but only in the continuation of life."*

## Self-Contemplation on the Inner Light

This contemplation will help you discern the truth about the Spiritual Hierarchy, the Heavenly Realms and your direct connection with Divine Spirit.

Select a room where you can be alone and undisturbed. Sit erect, comfortably, but do not lounge. Allow yourself 15 minutes to a half hour daily. Place your attention in the middle of your eye brows, your spiritual eye. Let your thoughts roam where they will but be perfectly still and watch for The Light within. (You may also hear what is known as The Sound Current, which will be explained later.) You may see a deep blue, violet, gold or white globe of Light, possibly a six-pointed star. This is perfectly normal as it is the *Inner Master, your true Self*-communicating with you. If you do, go with it and let it engulf you. Be very thankful, as you are truly blessed.

Continue this until you secure full control of your Physical Being. Listen to your breath. Does is sound smooth and silky or rough, like coarse sand paper? You know you are beginning to progress when the Physical body comes to stillness and the breathing is smooth as silk and relaxed.

In the beginning many will find this extremely difficult, while others will conquer it with ease, but it is absolutely essential to secure complete control of the Physical body before you are ready to progress.

# CHAPTER 4

## AWAKENING 3:
## POLARITY AND OPPOSITES

The first two awakenings always open the way for the next and if at any moment you need a refresher, just two words will do it: Source and Soul.

Understanding the principle of polarity helps you live a balanced life while in this world. A balanced life includes enthusiasm and contentment. You, Soul, can be "in this world but not of it." That is the key to understanding this principle and working with it instead of being controlled by it. The opposite polarities of light and dark, good and evil, wisdom and ignorance, youth and old age, govern this Physical world and all of the bodies residing here. That is why mastering your attitude and attention and keeping it polarized on Divine Spirit is so important.

Every manifestation, on whatever scale and in whatever world it may take place, from molecular to cosmic phenomena, is the result of combining the meeting of the two opposite forces of positive and negative, plus the third force, which is the passive middle. This is not the passive element that you find in negation, but a *balancing* of the two opposites.

Scientific thought today recognizes the existence of positive and negative forces and the necessity of the two for the production of phenomena; force and resistance, positive and negative magnetism, positive and negative electricity, male and female cells. But science has never raised the question of a third force. According to exact divine science, one force, or two forces, can never produce phenomena. The presence of the third is always necessary to produce any phenomenon. This neutral force is not easily accessible to direct observation and understanding. Mystics, saints and advanced Souls work knowingly with this neutral force.

You, as Soul, may have an awareness or memory that there are worlds where these polarities are not dominant. However, as long as You, Soul, are fixed to a Physical body, and have accepted a body, with or without responsibility, you are subjected to the polarities of this world and the forces that move through time, space, matter and energy.

You, as the individual Soul, going in and out of bodies, have collected a subconscious mind that is filled with the junk, negativity and the karmic burden from millions of lifetimes.

## Cause and Effect

If you want to cease being controlled by the polarities of this world and crush the karmic seeds so they no longer grow, *you must understand the distinction between living as cause or effect.*

When living as cause, you are truly "in this world but not of it" and expressing the creative principle. When living as effect, your life is mechanical instead of creative and the negative force controls your thoughts, emotions and actions. Although most humans are convinced that they are not controlled by the negative force, just look around and evidence of this is everywhere.

In the condition of being effect, you believe that someone or something has brought problems or happiness into your life. You believe that the swing of opposites happened *to you* and you are enslaved to reactive habits.

To free your mind and cease being the effect of the polarities in this Physical world begin to be aware of opposites in states of consciousness such as: praise or blame, contentment or dissatisfaction, interest or boredom, patience or frustration, and be aware if you are reacting to these states. The stronger the emotion, the more likely it is from the negative polarity.

It takes constant discernment, discipline and Divine Love to be cause instead of effect. Intellectuals may have discernment and discipline, however, it is the addition of Divine Love that liberates you, Soul, and so you can rise above polarities.

When you are *cause* you are aligned with Source Supreme and this brings positive experiences. When you are *effect* your experiences are controlled by dead energy flows and may be negative. (See the Chapter 7 on Facsimiles.) Living your life as either cause or effect depends on your attention and your spiritual progress and discipline.

A Physical example: Imagine you are near a swimming pool. You choose to sit on the edge of the pool and you put your feet into the water and make a conscious decision to enter the water. This is being *cause* and your experience is more likely to be positive. The opposite would be if you fall and stumble into the water, opening yourself to fear or panic. This is being *effect* and your experience is more likely to be negative.

Now consider this is also occurring in the Subtle Realms of the Astral, Causal, Mental and Etheric Realms, where you can also be cause or effect and why remaining aware and discerning at all times is so important.

*Discernment is essential because you as Soul can be aware of the experiences that are in harmony with Source Supreme and then live as cause instead of effect.*

By placing the all-powerful, all-knowing Divine Spirit, of which you are a part, behind your every thought, statement and action, and by always focusing on the "good," even when things appear to be going "badly," then in time, you will rise above the Law of Polarity. Everything is on a continuum and has an opposite.

You can transform undesirable thoughts by concentrating on the opposite pole. *For anything to exist, there has to be an equal and exact opposite.* Example: you cannot experience sadness without having an idea about happiness. Light cannot be experienced as such if you don't know darkness. To feel successful, you must know failure. Change an undesirable thought by concentrating on the opposite thought. This brings a desirable change in vibration and can be seen in positive life change.

When a Soul has gained perfect knowledge of being in harmony with Divine Spirit, the Law of Opposites does not affect IT. You walk through life in Divine Grace, the middle path of letting everything *Just Be.* You become a law unto your Self because you are in total harmony with the Source Supreme. Actually a better name for it is a *Balance* with all things. This is combining of the positive, negative and the neutral middle path.

It is the blending of the three currents into one that makes the whole man within this universe.

*"YOU of your Self can do nothing. Realize that The Source Supreme works through YOU in a balanced, detached way for the good of the Whole, from within to the outer world. Always place your attention on The Source Supreme and Divine Spirit."*

When one gains perfect knowledge of the Divine Spirit, you do not have to give up the Physical body and subtle bodies at once. You have the choice to continue living here as long as you are in perfect harmony with Divine Spirit as its agent and are not bothered with the Law of Opposites.

## Self-Contemplation on Polarity and Opposites

Go to your quiet place and take your accustomed position, close your eyes, take a deep breath and relax, let go. You want to reside in a balanced, relaxed and alert state of consciousness.

Read the following and ask to be shown who you truly are and how the creative power works. *Ask Divine Spirit for the knowledge and to show you how to consciously apply the law of three: positive, negative and passive neutral.*

A simple spiritual chemistry understanding: You are an exact replica of The Divine Source Supreme, an atom structure. The basic building blocks of all matter possess a positive charge, a negative charge or a neutral charge formed by the neutralization of positive and negative constituents. When particles join with each other through the reciprocal relationships of their dual characteristics, they form an atom.

Every atom has electrons, protons and neutrons. Electrons are negatively charged. Protons are positively charged. Neutrons are neutrally charged. Meaning, atoms are essentially energy. Atoms are balanced out by positive and negative charges. This is because they have the same number of protons (positive charges) and electrons (negative charges.) If an electron or proton is missing, you have a neutral charge. That's because the electrons and protons cancel themselves out and become a neutral charge.

For any Being to exist, energy is required, and energy can be produced only through give and take action. However, nothing can reciprocate without a partner. To generate the forces necessary for existence, a Being must contain dual characteristics, a subject partner and an object partner, which can engage in give and take action. You want to operate from Tuzashottama energy. This is the neutral energy that you will realize is developed by Soul, and all is guided, has its motion, and manifests from within.

When you resonate with the frequency of Divine Spirit you actually begin to dwell in the Heavenly Realms while still on Earth. When you shed your Physical body, you will make a smooth translation, with no fear and great confidence about your place and purpose in the Heavenly Worlds.

Soul, your true spiritual Self, would be a neutral charge with all the electrons and protons in the molecules balancing the charges of positive and negative. Therefore, You, Soul, would be *a state of being* that is neutrally charged and can accomplish and manifest your desires in the Dense and Subtle Realms, as well as in the Heavenly Realms. Your goal would be *balance,* neither for, nor against, operating from your true Self, Soul.

Once you know and understand Polarity and Opposites let your daily thoughts dwell upon your ideal as an already existing fact:

- If you wish to eliminate fear, bring a relaxed state of concentration onto courage.

- To eliminate lack, bring a relaxed state of concentration onto abundance.

- If you wish to eliminate disease, bring a relaxed state of concentration onto health.

*Always* see and feel the end result as an already existing fact.

Your breathing and posture greatly influence your state of consciousness. If you need help in achieving this state of relaxed concentration you can experiment with visualizing smiley faces throughout your body to help you gain the ideal balance of relaxation and concentration. Through consistent practice of the Self-Contemplations, this state of relaxed concentration becomes more natural.

# CHAPTER 5

## AWAKENING 4:
## VIBRATIONS AND HARMONICS

Advanced Beings understand the importance of awakening to a deep understanding of how vibrations and harmonics govern all the influences upon us as a Soul living in a Physical body. The vibrations flowing through this world from the planets, stars, music, sound and color penetrate all Beings and it is up to each of us to be discerning about what we allow into our eternal life.

As a Being seeking awakening and true understanding of who and what we are, one of the most important realizations to embrace is that we are totally responsible for our experiences and the vibrations we allow in and through us. This means we take full responsibility for everything we think and say and do and learn to be the conscious cause in our lives rather than the effect of what comes our way. It means giving our attention to that which is in perfect accord with Source Supreme and Soul.

While some may view being totally responsible as a daunting concept, it is actually the good news. Imagine; if you are totally responsible for your vibrations, then you have the power to create a life that is positive, uplifting, joyous and filled with love and grace. Because you have the ability to change your vibrations you can change your life.

You have the power to attract wonderful experiences, abundance, and what some refer to as miracles and sweet moments of Divine Love, those extraordinary moments when we feel completely connected with the Heavenly Nectar, the Light and Sound.

This has been written about for hundreds of years in mystical writings and sacred scriptures. Today and over the past several decades it has been emphasized to the point where it is heard constantly in popular books, music and movies, so why is positive change so difficult for many?

Everyone wants to be happy, yet for most it is elusive. Remember, we have discussed the extreme propaganda and deceptiveness prevalent in this Kali Yuga that keep the vibrations anchored to lower frequencies. Protecting yourself using the "White Light Technique" provides the power you need to raise your vibrations.

All thoughts, words and actions transmit a vibration on a scale from utterly uplifting to devastatingly destructive. Like invisible radio frequency waves that issue forth into the ethers, we constantly transmit vibrations that tell the universe what we want, what we love and what we want to express and experience.

In response to our invisible message to the universe, we connect with that which is in accord with our state of consciousness. What returns to us is in harmony with our vibration. The energetic signature we leave as footprints on the shores of the spiritual ocean that supplies and sustains all life, returns to us that which we silently ask for.

## Karmic Healing

This is where an understanding of karma is necessary. All thoughts, feelings, words and actions create a karmic "etch" or engraving, sometimes called an engram or a samsaric impression. The karmic impressions that are most dominant have the strongest engraving and have been with you for lifetimes.

*Karma is not a reward or punishment.* Because we live in a mathematical universe, your dominant karmic impressions direct your behavior and shape your worldview. This is why you sometimes say or do things that you later regret or call an "error." The karmic impressions are stored in the causal body and subconscious mind. The old karmic patterns can pull you to repeat negative habits in a self-perpetuating, self-induced state of hypnosis until you have help in breaking free. Karma is also created with all current activity of your body, mind and speech.

Resist the temptation to criticize or look down upon yourself or others when you observe the karmic suffering of illness or poverty. Difficult karma is asking for compassion and wisdom via thought, word and action. A wise teacher once said: "Compassion is the place where your love touches the pain of another; pity is the place where your fear touches the pain of another."

Karma is often spoken of as seeds – "as you sow, so shall ye reap." This helps us understand that only an apple seed produces an apple tree. Only seeds of poison ivy can produce a poison ivy bush. The karmic seeds we sow are usually a large mix that brings forth fields of both happiness and suffering. *No one other than us can sow seeds into our field of consciousness.* Most people's lives are like fields with apple trees, flowers, weeds and vines of poison ivy, all growing together in one lifetime.

Since karma does carry forward from past lifetimes, it can appear mysterious. *"Who would ever sow such a seed to have this in my life,"* is a common question. Denial, guilt, anger and blaming others for our current life conditions are common Human maladies. When this arises, return to the Self-Contemplations on *forgiveness.* There is also family, generational and cultural karma that impacts our lives so the best approach is to be gentle while still moving forward with your head up and eyes wide open.

How quickly karma ripens depends on the causes and conditions of each seed planted. One of the primary benefits of awakening is to learn to protect yourself and others from the negative karma of this Kali Yuga. You can learn to crush the seeds of karma before they ripen by practicing the Self-Contemplations outlined in this book.

When you place your attention on Divine Spirit and ask for help in moving into the Heavenly Worlds, clearing negativity from your life may come at a fast pace and could be overwhelming. Please remember that *you are always in control* and directly ask Divine Spirit to slow it down if need be. The Self Contemplations offer you a "lifeline" to lift you up and out of the karmic net.

## The Power of Attraction

Some spiritual teachings emphasize gathering positive karma or merit. What this accomplishes is that your vibrations are refined and *attract* people and conditions that are filled with positive spiritual energy. Your good karma can bring you into close contact with advanced Spiritual Initiates or a true Spiritual Master.

Sages have said that good karma is like a golden chain and negative karma is like barbed wire, both bind the Soul to the dense energy realms. To become free, you awaken to the Source Supreme and devote your life to being an agent for Divine Love, so you cease creating karma.

At that point you have a choice in every moment of your life to connect with and express the highest vibrations of Divine Unconditional Love and live a life in harmony with the Light and Sound.

When we live a life in harmony with the higher frequencies of Light and Sound, we attract Divine Spirit, which is a transformative force that will benefit and truly contribute to the healing of all beings in all worlds.

Just like tuning in to a radio signal, we have the ability to tune into higher frequencies by using our faculties to speak sacred words, visualize and imagine we are in communication with those sacred Beings, visible and invisible, who can connect us with the Light and Sound ~ the frequency that is the direct road into the heart of God, the Source Supreme.

*Consider that spirituality is caught not taught.* This means that connecting with the vibration that is the God current and filling our minds and hearts with the Light that is the manifestation of the presence of God/ Source Supreme, is choosing to be who we truly are and living in our true home.

We must also remember that our vibration is a result of that which we attract into our sphere of action via our attention. Just as the Light and Sound are food for Soul and can raise our vibration, those things we listen to or view can also penetrate into our energetic body and raise or even lower our vibration. What raises or lowers our vibration creates a cause attracting to us that, which is in harmony with that vibration.

It is critically important that we consciously choose the music we listen to, the movies and television we watch, and most importantly, the people we invite into our company. Music can affect our mood and uplift our hearts and help us to soar heavenward. It has been used purposefully in movies and television to create an atmosphere.

All we observe and wherever we invest our time and attention affects our personal atmosphere. Music and imagery alike can fill us with a fragrant perfume or a lingering stench and can open us to sublime experiences or that which is frightening and negative.

The spiritual practices offered here are specifically presented to lead you into the Higher Realms, clear away negative karmic residue, and connect you with the Light and Sound and protection so you may travel into the Heart of IT and dwell in the presence of Source Supreme.

## Self-Contemplation on Vibrations and Harmonics

The Ancient Spiritual Masters taught the *Study of Sound* before any of the other studies of Divine Spirit. They were aware, through their personal study and research that all sound vibrations came from the *Original Sound Current of Source Supreme.* They also realized that these vibrations could be altered and deflected. They blended this knowledge into a special formula that has been preserved into modern times. This formula is known as the seven-tone scale; therefore music became the first of the art forms in the Physical and Subtle Realms. This seven-tone scale is also the sacred formula of the universe and is connected to the seven spiritual steams that separate from the Original Prime Sound Current.

Vibrations and Harmonics govern all the influences upon you, Soul, and the Physical body in this world. Music, color, wavelengths, frequencies, and sound fall under the principle of karma, cause and effect; inflow and outflow as explained earlier in this chapter.

Have you ever heard a ringing or high-pitched electrical sound in your head or your ears? This is natural; it is the Force of life, the rushing of atoms of the Sound Current. Earlier we mentioned the various Spiritual Planes or Dimensions. Each Plane has a particular sound associated with its own frequency or vibration. These sounds act as a "road map," and an identifying placement of where your attention is at a particular moment.

The Original Sound Current issuing forth from Source Supreme is the all pervading, purifying, Spiritual Current that brings new life to Soul, allowing us to gain the Heavenly Worlds in this lifetime. The Sound Current is a cleansing agent for all the Worlds and the creative force that lifts each of us into the Higher worlds of Source Supreme, This is our true mission; liberation of Soul here, now.

## Source Supreme

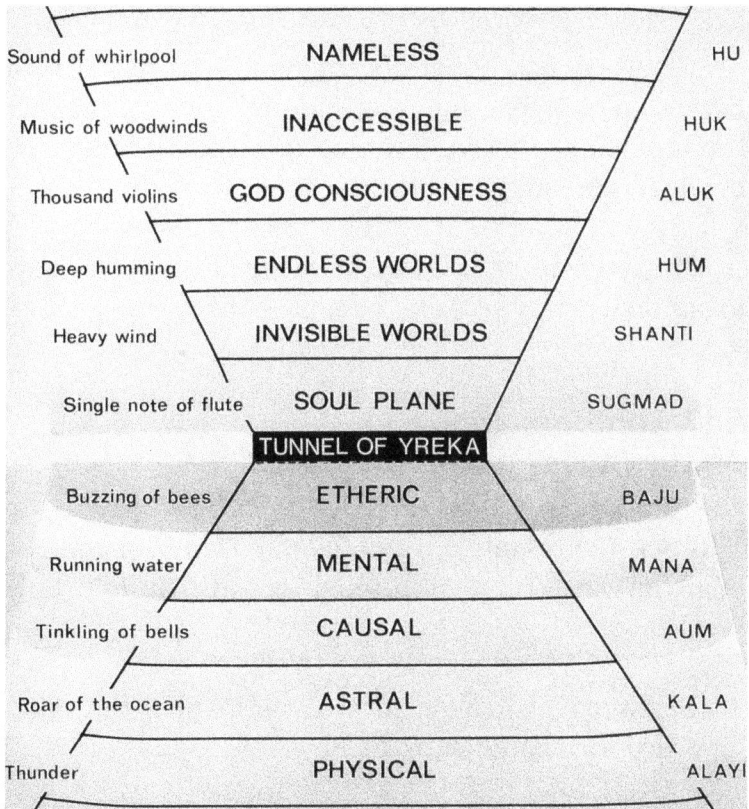

| Sound | Plane | Word |
|---|---|---|
| Sound of whirlpool | NAMELESS | HU |
| Music of woodwinds | INACCESSIBLE | HUK |
| Thousand violins | GOD CONSCIOUSNESS | ALUK |
| Deep humming | ENDLESS WORLDS | HUM |
| Heavy wind | INVISIBLE WORLDS | SHANTI |
| Single note of flute | SOUL PLANE | SUGMAD |
| | TUNNEL OF YREKA | |
| Buzzing of bees | ETHERIC | BAJU |
| Running water | MENTAL | MANA |
| Tinkling of bells | CAUSAL | AUM |
| Roar of the ocean | ASTRAL | KALA |
| Thunder | PHYSICAL | ALAYI |

Go to your room where you will not be disturbed, sit erect in your chair and place your attention on your spiritual eye (the spot between your brow.) Take some very deep breaths and relax. Now slowly move your attention into the middle of your head, the part of the brain known as the pineal gland.

*You may ask "what does a gland have to do with Divine Spirit?" The pineal gland acts as a *vibrational receptor* for sacred information and knowledge between the Physical body and Soul.

*The realization that we are Divine Beings, Soul, rests in our own hands here and now.*

## Self-Contemplation
## on the Inner Realms or Dimensions

This Self-Contemplation can be practiced in segments, or all the way through the Dimensions into the Heavenly Worlds.

1   Begin to sing in a long drawn out manner the word associated with the Physical Plane –
ALAYI

*Ahaaa-Lay-Yeee; repeat this three times and pay attention to how you feel. Sit in silence; focus on this Physical song of Divine Spirit. You may hear and actually feel the sound of Thunder run up your spine into your head.*

2   Next sing the word associated with the Astral
    Plane – KALA. Sing it 3 times: KaaaaLaaaa.
    Watch, listen and sense the subtle Divine
    Light increase in intensity and hear sound of
    *the Ocean.* (Science refers to this Plane as the
    Troposphere.)

    *You can do these song gems of Divine Spirit for
    several days or weeks before going up the tone
    scale to the Higher Planes. There is no rush. You
    will be guided if you pay attention.*

3   When you feel that you are ready, now sing the
    word of the Causal Plane – AUM - 3 times and
    listen. AaaaaaaaaUmmmmmmm. The Light
    should be brighter and the sound is *Tinkling
    Bells.* (Scientifically this Plane corresponds
    to the Tropopause.) You should have a
    knowingness of expanding in consciousness.
    Do not let your thoughts drift. Keep your
    attention on the Light and Sound of this Plane.

4   The Mental Plane (Stratosphere) is a vast
    universe of enchantment and beauty; therefore
    you must be aware of hypnotic or mesmerizing
    traps that will want to keep you there. The
    word you sing is MANA – MaaaaNnnnnAaaaa.
    The sound associated with the Mental
    Dimension is *Running Water.*

    *To manage your mind, know that there is nothing
    and relinquish all attachment to the nothingness.*

5   The next Plane is the Etheric (ionosphere).
    This Plane is the communicator between Dense
    Realm bodies and you, Soul, and the Heavenly
    Worlds. Sing BAJU – BaaaaJuuuuu - 3 or more
    times. Be still and listen for the sound of
    *Buzzing of Bees.*

6   You now are going to enter the Soul Plane
    where your true knowledge of Source Supreme
    begins. This is the dividing Plane between the
    psychic and the true spiritual worlds. You will
    become refined, civilized, and have Compassion
    and Divine Love for all life... for you will
    realize that we are all One. Sing SUGMAD –
    SuuuugMaaad - 6 to 12 times. You will be truly
    blessed hearing the *Single Note of a Flute or
    high-pitch electrical sound.*

    *True Realization comes from direct merger of
    one's Being with the Divine energy of the Source
    Supreme.*

## Special Instructions

You may visit each Plane separately, contemplate and
learn the information the particular frequency gives
you, or you may sing them in order about 3 times each,
taking a deep breath in-between each word song going
up the scale reaching the Soul Plane. By singing these
sacred words over the weeks and months, you will find
that you will heal your Physical, Astral, Causal, Mental

and Etheric Bodies. You will begin to operate from your true Self, Soul, and have many Self and God realizations.

You will also begin your Awakening in the Dream Conscious State. When you are ready you will enter the Heavenly Worlds. There are at least five more Heavenly World Dimensions that are out-of-body Dimensions, which will be mentioned, in a later chapter.

Each of these Realms, from the Dense, to the Subtle to the higher Heavenly Worlds is a subjective and objective reality. While visiting these worlds, you may also experience meeting with a True Spiritual Master and You, Soul, can be given instructions either individually or in a group in a Luminous Wisdom Temple.

Remember, Questions are unnecessary. You cannot have a Question without already having the Answer. *All Answers lie within you. Be Still and Know.*

# CHAPTER 6

## AWAKENING 5:
## ATTITUDE AND ATTENTION

*Attitude and Attention are the key secrets of your Spiritual growth and conscious awareness. The chief delusion is that there are causes at work in your life other than your own state of consciousness. All that happens to you, all that is done by you, comes to you as a result of your own state of consciousness. This is also true of your own state of spiritual consciousness, for you are all that you think, desire and love, all you believe to be true and consent to, will happen to you.*

The natural progression of awakening flows from Vibrations and Harmonics to Attitude and Attention. Your attitude transmits a vibration and moves in a positive direction as you invoke Source Supreme to guide you until you attain an attitude of childlike curiosity and reliance on Divine Spirit. The longer you sustain this childlike attitude, with your attention firmly held on Divine Love, the more you attract peace, health, love, joy and prosperity.

*What stands between you and this childlike attitude is fear that your needs will not be met and this fear creates anxiety and unhealthy competition, closing the channel to Divine Spirit, binding you to the lower emotional plane.*

*Know that the real you, Soul, can never die as we understand dying in the Physical Realm. Soul is eternal and has no beginning or ending. Soul always lives in the present, for it has no past or future.*

Cultural conditioning and propaganda in the Kali Yuga send constant messages to make you feel insecure. Insecurity intensifies tension; tension arises from fear; fear rises out of excessive self-grasping; excessive self-grasping cuts one off from the flow of Divine Spirit, thus, the qualities leading to satisfaction, happiness and growth are not achieved.

When you realize that you have immeasurable value and importance to the Source Supreme, you naturally relax. You cease grasping and clinging to things before others can have them, tensions subside, and you open to receive the blessings of Divine Spirit. You are free from the rigidity of negative emotions and can rise to the spiritual planes where life flows with grace.

True openness and relaxation flow from the childlike attitude, and all channels from within are opened. Without causing harm to anyone, the Spirit of you reaches out in Spirit, touching the Spirit of those who are positioned to help fulfill your needs, and increases your ability for helping yourself and others.

Many people want this confidence that they are connected to Source Supreme and to all Souls, but conditioning and long standing karmic habits make it a challenge.

It is time to awaken to the power of a corrected attitude and give your attention to Source Supreme. The spiritual attitude is about corrected feelings and pictures constantly held in your mind. When you take a picture with a camera ~ let's say of a flower, and do so, you view the flower in the viewfinder. Sometimes when you look at the picture you've taken, it is crystal clear, other times it is blurry and you need to adjust the focus. Adjusting the focus on a camera is like adjusting your attention to be sure you have the correct picture held steadily in your mind.

When we think of something and hold a strong emotion along with the thought, we are sighting pictures in the viewfinder of the mind. Sometimes we make an error with taking a picture with a camera and realize we had the camera pointed away from what we want. It is similar with our mind pictures.

It is most important to realize that we are taking millions of mind pictures each day, so it is no wonder we need to understand how to best focus our attitude and attention correctly.

This awareness helps you understand that you are fully responsible for all of the experiences in your life. There are no excuses to be made. Although an undisciplined mind can be influenced to focus on negativity, it is still up to you to refocus your attention and not blame others for "doing things to you."

Of course there are events that occur in the world where we see or hear about people or animals being hurt and it is healthy and natural to feel sad or angry and even shed some tears of compassion. Some of us have a role in the world to protect those who are suffering and stand up against injustice. How we do this opens us to become a channel either for Divine Spirit or the negative force. An individual who has trained their consciousness toward Divine Spirit is resilient and the attention returns to a place of optimism and positive action without dwelling on negative emotions because we can do more good in the world when we act as a channel for Source Supreme.

By holding the attention on the corrected pictures in your mind, you choose to be happy, joyful and at peace. Your attention can cause you to experience the bliss of the Source Supreme and dwell in the Heavenly Realms. Or, conversely, your attention can pull you into negative states of sadness, self-pity, bitterness, and even hate. Think about this: Where you place your attention directly affects your attitude and in every moment it is your choice.

For example, take a moment to reflect on some of your own personal experiences. First remember a sweet and precious moment with someone you love. Let the feeling of that memory fill your being. How do you feel?

Now bring your attention to a moment that was upsetting to you. Perhaps you had a quarrel or even a loss of some kind. How do you feel?

Now remember a wonderful celebration. Perhaps it was your birthday, your wedding, or a wonderful accomplishment. How do you feel?

What you have just done is to consciously affect your own attitude based on where you placed your attention. This is the way to that childlike attitude that brings the greatest blessings.

It is natural for human beings to develop habits and so often behavior becomes subconscious and repetitive. This can be either positive or negative. Since our attitude and attention truly are our own responsibility and can be directed by conscious choice, it is important to create new, healthy habits.

Another way to understand this is to view your physical body as the "vehicle" like a car that Soul uses to navigate and travel in this Physical world. You, as Soul are supposed to be the driver of this vehicle. When you drive your car, you are in control of steering your vehicle just as you are in control of steering your Physical vehicle into positive or negative territory. If you are reckless, drunk or fall asleep at the wheel of your Physical car, what happens is still your responsibility. It is the same with you as Soul.

When driving a car, if you want to make a turn you move the wheel to the right or left. If you want to go straight ahead, you keep the wheels of the car going forward by adjusting ever so slightly even if the wheels of the car are pulling to the right or left.

In the same way, when the mind and thoughts are joyful or happy or even neutral you are a channel for Divine Love. However, when your thoughts and emotions are turbulent, this is where discipline and discernment matter most. It is important to practice the Self-Contemplations given in this book so that you can quickly rebound from negative thoughts. Just as a skilled driver can correct the steering of a car, you can correct your mind pictures and shift your attention to positive thoughts, images and memories.

*"Energy flows where attention goes."* This means that you bring to life, or animate that experience or idea where you invest your precious attention. When you fill your attention with uplifting ideas, images and memories, and connect with the Light and Sound you invite those experiences into your reality.

Previously in this book we mentioned that this is a mathematical universe, so remember that success in attracting that which you choose depends on the quality and quantity of attention you invest.

Practicing the Self-Contemplations on a daily basis will help you create a new habit of returning to a state of consciousness that is positive, creative and filled with the Light and Sound of Source Supreme. It takes constant and dedicated vigilance and with continued practice can bring a most wonderful result transforming you, blessing your life and touching everyone you meet.

When you practice continuously, you create the new habit of keeping the attitude and attention positive. The more you practice, the easier and more natural it becomes. Then the fragrance of your Being and your vibration become harmonized with Source Supreme. When you are living in harmony with Source Supreme you will radiate a glow that others will perceive and that will help them connect to the Light and Sound. This is what it means to be a vehicle for Source Supreme and to dwell in the Pure Positive Worlds making your life a living example of Divine Love.

## Self-Contemplation on Attitude and Attention

This will be a most powerful Self-Contemplation as your *Attitude* and *Attention* is the basis of all spiritual endeavors.

Your thoughts produce a certain vibratory rate that enters the formless (Divine Spirit) and take form somewhere in the Universes of the Source Supreme. These will return to you some day, somewhere in time. Not only will they return to your own personal universe, but these thoughts, either positive or negative, will also affect the Universal atmosphere and environment. Positive, pleasant, and beautiful thoughts attract more of the same and grow in scope. Negative, sad, or bitter thoughts do the same. The tendency will be to increase whatever you choose.

It is for this reason that great spiritual teachers have constantly warned their students to keep thoughts pleasant and harmonious *with all life.*

Remember that *Attention* intensifies and *Attitude* determines the result. It has been said "Silent thought is the mightiest agent in Human affairs."

This Self-Contemplation will have multi-lessons woven throughout, so be very aware of what you can learn from it.

Go to your usual place, take a comfortable position in your chair, take some deep breaths and let go of your day's affairs. Place your attention on your spiritual eye, then move it to the middle of your brain cavity. Now move your attention to the top of your head, the Crown Chakra. How do you feel?

Concentrate on a spot on the ceiling about 5-to-10 feet above your head. Move your attention from your Crown Chakra to that spot and look down upon the top of your head and view your Physical body and the room where you are sitting. Look around with your Spiritual Eyes. Really look and study everything from Soul.

Now move in Soul further away from your Physical body going higher and higher viewing the rooftop of your house. You have no limitations. Look at your neighborhood. See the trees, the grass, the birds, etc. Send forth Divine Love and Good Will. Be thankful.

Now continue to expand as you move higher in Soul viewing planet Earth. Look with your spiritual eyes from Soul and examine the beautiful planets and stars. Send forth and express Gratitude, Divine Love and Good Will to all of Source Supreme. *Know* that there are other Souls that will accept your Divine Love and Good Will.

Are you beginning to realize who and what you are? How powerful you are? How magnificent, beautiful and wonderful you are? You have all the attributes of the Divine Source Supreme. You are Omnipotent, Omniscient, and Omnipresent!

Knowing that you are an exact duplicate, in Soul, of the Source Supreme, a microcosm of the macrocosm you have no limitations.

You can instantly direct-project via Soul anywhere, anytime: *Be, Look, Know.*

Realize that You are a multi-dimensional Being consciously operating from your true Self, Soul.

When ready, gently return to the Physical body. Relax and ponder your uplifting experience.

To be spiritually free from all limitations, deny the evidence of the outer senses and begin to feel subjectively the joy of BEING FREE. By realizing that you are an exact replicate of the Source Supreme you uplift the consciousness of all Souls in all the worlds of Source Supreme. Simply stated: Just BE!

# CHAPTER 7

## AWAKENING 6: FACSIMILES

Awakening to the truth about *Facsimiles* is essential in understanding why some have great success when applying "the law of attraction" and others say it doesn't work for them.

In the Physical world a *Facsimile* is referred to as making an exact duplicate or replicate of something. In the Spiritual world it is a thought form that is also a duplicate. It can be a duplicate of an original thought form from Source Supreme, or a thought form from your stored karmic impressions or a thought form from someone else that you have accepted as your own.

Facsimiles are units of energy, little pictures that surround the body, the mind and Soul that have been gathered around you since birth. When Soul views them, they can either be pleasant (positive) or they can be troublesome (negative.) These units of energy are past or current karmic impressions or engrams, and one way or another they will influence you. If negative, a Facsimile *can control your mind causing a downward spiral* into emotional problems with various aberrations affecting all your actions including a variety of unwanted health issues.

The good news is that Facsimiles are dead flow energy units and can be overwritten or neutralized. What keeps them alive is attention from both the conscious and subconscious habits of body, mind and speech. By consciously placing your *attention* on the positive opposite of a negative picture the karma can be subdued or eliminated and the negative behaviors will cease, often in a way that seems miraculous. You will observe that your breathing patterns change, your voice becomes more natural and relaxed and your body movements become powerful.

Those who are called mystics, saints, or seers have the ability to see these energy units and have been known to offer help in resolving negative energy flows. What we are offering here is a way for you to empower yourself so you will not need to rely on anyone to give you a reading or a clearing or anything designed to remove these negative conditions. The more you awaken to your direct connection to Source Supreme, the sooner you will be living fully as a liberated, self-realized Soul.

The Self-Contemplations, when practiced consistently, dissolve the karmic patterns that are stored in the subconscious mind and Causal body and the aberrant behavior decreases until it is gone. Remember, karma can be subdued and crushed. (Refer to Chapter 4 on Opposites and Polarity.)

*If you are reading this book and not practicing the Self-Contemplations, it is like buying an exercise book full of descriptions and pictures of physical weight lifting but not engaging in the actual practice. Reading alone is not enough to gain physical, mental or spiritual power.*

## Self-Contemplation on Facsimiles

You can overwrite and eliminate these dead pictures of Facsimiles by replacing them with the opposite positive virtues. This particular Self-Contemplation may take several weeks, so be patient. The results will be worth your effort.

Go to your quiet room, sit upright in your chair and take some deep breaths. Relax you entire Physical body. Now gently direct your attention to your spiritual eye (the point between the eyebrows) and then move that attention to the middle of your head.

We begin this Self-Contemplation by examining the 5 passions of the mind: Anger, Attachment, Greed, Lust and Vanity.

Begin today with *Anger.* Ask yourself "what *Angers* you?" Who, what, when, where and why? Remember, this may take some time. Be specific. *Forgive,* and replace this mind passion with Divine Love. Really mean it and let go. When you feel you have conquered this passion, move on to the next one and begin by asking yourself "what am I *attached* to?" This does not mean that you must give up your family, friends and loved ones or even your personal possessions. It means can you walk away from something without regrets.

Now take a look at *Greed,* then *Lust,* and then *Vanity* in the same manner. Replace them with their opposites.

In your everyday life talk to people about respecting their Parents, Grandparents, Senior Citizens, Animals and a basic love for all life.

The Native American Hopi Indians, in their sacred writings practiced the following peace-loving principles. All should practice these peace-loving principles:

- Live simply and don't let materialism control your life.

- Teach your children to respect others.

- Guard against anger, and unhappy thoughts.

- Watch your language! Use words to uplift, encourage and inspire, not to tear down.

- Be self-sufficient. Do not depend upon others for your personal survival.

- Recognize temptation when you see it. Be suspicious of anything that glitters with charm.

Remember nothing in life is free, there is always a price to pay.

The *love of all life* is the most enriching and rewarding of all spiritual virtues. It streams into the world through the Souls that are more open to the influence of Divine Spirit as a channel from the heart of Source Supreme. When one becomes receptive to ITS gentle influence and sustenance, IT sustains all with ITS redeeming power, and heals the wounds and restores the awareness of Divine Benevolence.

You must work honestly within your Self to gain a high degree of ethics and standards. *You must be a law unto your Self.* YOU must walk this spiritual path alone. No one can do it for you. As you unfold spiritually and enter the Higher Realms, more knowledge is given to you and you become more humble and thankful. You are Awakening, eliminating fear, and will realize your true mission this lifetime.

# CHAPTER 8

## AWAKENING 7: UNITY

*Awakening to Unity completes the circle that began with the first Awakening.*

Much has been written stating that we are all connected, yet to understand this at the Soul level is the final liberation from fear and brings us into full Self Realization.

When you think and visualize in the whole, instead of in parts, there is a constant awareness of Source Supreme enlivening you, Soul. This is the awakening to unity. The solution to any problem is then known in an instant when you fully awaken to your relationship to Source Supreme and all Souls.

In this density with polarities of light and dark, especially during the Kali Yuga, it is challenging to look beyond the layers of karmic knots and see each other as whole, radiant and divine and remain aware of our unity.

Through daily practice of Self-Contemplations, we see, feel, accept and treat all Souls and ourselves with Divine Love. This does not mean we abandon boundaries and this is subtle. We continue to use protection practices until our radiance is so brilliant that everyone we meet recognizes us as Soul and would never want to harm us. Or we become invisible to those who are practicing negativity.

It is a great law of life that all Souls are precious and the greatest commandments have emphasized how to give Divine Love and wish all Souls to be fully awake in the presence of Source Supreme. Whatever you wish for yourself, either consciously or subconsciously, vibrates out to all Souls in all Realms.

## Collective Consciousness

In each era and time period, there is a collective consciousness in the world. The Souls living in a given time and geographical area are connected to the karmic conditions of that time and place. This includes health and illness, poverty and abundance, and war or peace. Some illness and suffering comes into a given area and time as part of a karmic cleansing, in the same way that rain storms clear the air over our Earth. This is not a punishment; it is a healing and resolution. Some religious groups mistakenly believe it is God's wrath, however, it is the coalescence of thought and emotion by the Souls dwelling in the Physical, Astral, Causal and Mental Realms. Not all illness and suffering is due to individual karma, as the group consciousness of the time plays a role in what happens to each Soul.

This is why you must use great discernment in joining any religious, political or professional group. Group thought can be powerful and unless Divine Love for the good of all Souls guides it, it can be dangerous. When Souls come together in genuine friendship, harmony and understanding, darkness is dispelled and each individual light shines more brightly.

Some of you are familiar with the spiritual terms of "Satsang and Sangha." These terms refer to groups that are gathered in the name of Divine Love and when a True Spiritual Master guides them, they do tremendous good in all worlds. However, in this Kali Yuga it is rare to find an authentic master. We have emphasized the importance of You, Soul, in taking responsibility for your awakening and your physical life without needing to rely on anyone by practice of the Self-Contemplations offered here.

## Awakening To Unity

Awakening to unity allows you to meet life in a relaxed manner. It is being like a fish swimming with the ocean current. You don't want to struggle and fight the current or sink down to the bottom in a lifeless, apathetic manner. It is a balance between effort and grace. Your effort while in these dualistic Realms propels you forward and Divine Grace, which continually flows from the Source, is your invisible ally. You cannot overly use one without the other.

*It is possible for one to be a channel of the Divine Spirit through belief and strong feelings.* By this method alone can wonders be worked, for words and actions will be of great power, and when one feels strongly about this there can be nothing in this world which can shake you of this faith. Then belief becomes a powerful conviction. Every spiritual giant, saint, and adept has had this faith of conviction.

This creates a vibration of its own, an atmosphere around you, which will continue to grow until others start noticing it, and your growth will be in leaps and bounds.

You should have a good picture of the Real Self, the individual that is really you, Soul. Yes, it is also vital to have a good clear picture, an absolute conviction of the resources of the Divine Spirit. This Spirit is endless, limitless and all encompassing. All things pour forth from this great intelligence, this Source Supreme. Once you realize this, once you have a vivid mental picture of this limitless power and might, once you visualize it you naturally have complete confidence in it and then wonders begin to happen.

*The secret of awakening to unity lies in the fact that any problem the individual has, is always a personal problem. Since Divine Power is infallible, that is, incapable of making an error, it is the individual use of this power that creates the errors.*

To use the power correctly requires absolute trust in the Source Supreme and acceptance that there will always be the assistance you need in your life. If you rely too strongly on a few people and become rigid in thinking that only these few can help you, then true unity is not lighting your way to the Heavenly Realms.

For instance, if you need a ride to the airport, or to a doctor's appointment, or a referral to help grow your business, be open that there is a Soul somewhere who hears your call for help the moment you put it forth. We covered how to hold the corrected feeling in the chapters on Attitudes and Facsimiles, so if questions arise now, review those chapters.

Some have misunderstood the truth of unity because of new-age myths and pop psychology and they go to extremes with no planning and say, "Oh, I've surrendered it to Spirit" and they neglect responsibility for paying their own way in this world. This is not awakening to unity, it is foolishness. The truth of this is revealed the more you deepen your daily practice and rise up to express acts of power, usefulness and beauty.

## Self-Contemplation on Unity

Take your seat as usual. Take several breaths and sit up straight and relax your entire body into stillness. Begin by asking yourself: "What would my life be like, at home, at work and socially, if I never again said or thought anything to elevate myself by putting someone else down." This practice brings to awareness how often we create separation by thinking of ourselves as kinder, smarter, more committed to health, or more responsible, etc. This thinking shows up in how we think and speak about people of different race, religion, and in today's world especially about differing political views. Each thought, word and deed that elevates us by putting someone else down is a barrier to being connected to the Source Supreme. It is propaganda that is prevalent in today's world and is most insidious, so this requires deep reflection.

Now that you know the Truth, begin to imagine a situation where you have needed assistance in some way and it didn't show up. It could be something physical such as repairing something broken like a computer or a car, or emotional support in showing of affection, or mental in helping to understand a difficult concept. It could be because you were too proud or frightened to ask for help or the person you asked just let you down. Visualize the experience moving farther and farther into the past and say to yourself, "I can hardly remember when that happened" and exhale with a sigh as you release the memory. Continue and say, I am now fully awakened to the Source Supreme, and I see the Soul who is there for me, holding my hand and we walk into the light together. You don't need to put a face or name to the Soul helping you, imagine it as a protective, wise and caring Soul showing up just as you need them.

# CHAPTER 9

## AWAKENING 10: DIVINE LOVE

Do you remember *The Golden Rule* passed down through the eons of time? *"Do unto others that which you would have them do unto you."*

This statement is most important and another key to the mechanics of Self Mastery. It serves as a warning. A fundamental truth of caution. Your Consciousness *is* Source Supreme, God, the one and only reality. The giver of all gifts.

This is the oneness of life. Understand that desires, regardless of their nature, are easily expressed and manifested with the sacred knowledge. *Whatever you feel and believe to be true of yourself or another should be considered a gift.* What you feel and believe to be true of another is a gift you have given to them. The gift always returns to the sender, the giver. If you fix a belief within yourself, this unaccepted gift will return and embody itself within your world. *Only accept such states as true of others that you would willingly accept as true of yourself.*

Suggestions, prayers and wishes are like propaganda. They are boomerangs unless those to whom they are sent accept them. Remember the Law of Oneness; your world is a gift you have given to your Self. Discover and fully realize the law of Oneness, One Consciousness, and you will live by the Golden Rule and know the Kingdom of Heaven is within and objectified without. This is Divine Love for all life.

*A wise and disciplined Soul obeys The Golden Rule. It is good common sense.*

When all is distilled down to its prime origin we find Love at the source. As Human Beings we can experience Love in many forms. There is that warm love we feel for those closest to us, those in our inner circle; there is the love and affection for those we share life experiences with on a wider scale and there is love for other creatures, for nature, our activities, and many things we experience in this life.

Each of us has experienced Human love in one form or another. Some of us have experienced a different love ~ Divine Love ~ a spiritual Love for God and all creation that exists beyond worldly description or limitation. It is an undeniable power that opens us to broader planes and higher visions and quenches that eternal thirst to know who and what we are, what our purpose is, where we came from and where we are going.

Love is that invisible force which connects us heart to heart and Soul-to-Soul. Love can find us and penetrate deeply into the inner recesses of our being lighting up our entire consciousness. The quality of Divine Love is so powerful as to ignite a fire within that can lead us to remember who we really are and that our true home is in the heart of God THE SOURCE SUPREME.

When the hunger for finding our true home is awakened, we become insatiable for connection with the Divine Current, which can be recognized in the twin aspects of Light and Sound.

So what can we do to nurture the flame of Divine Love and reconnect with the Light and Sound to tread the path into the heart of the Source Supreme and find our way back to our true home?

Practicing the Law of Divine Love and Giving is very simple: if you want joy and happiness, give joy and happiness to others; if you want Divine Love, learn to give Divine Love; if you want material affluence, help others to become materially affluent. In fact, the easiest way to get what you want is to help others get what they want. Bless everyone silently with all the good things in life. Bless them that their consciousness will be open to accept the Divine understanding of their true purpose.

Make a decision that any time you come into contact with anyone, you will give him or her something. It doesn't have to be in the form of material things; it could be a flower, a compliment, or sending a wave of Divine Love. In fact, the most powerful forms of giving are non-material. The gifts of caring, attention, a positive attitude, affection, appreciation, and Divine Love are the most precious gifts you can give. When you meet someone, you can silently send him or her a silent blessing, happiness and Divine Love.

*This kind of silent giving is very powerful.*

Our true nature is one of affluence and abundance; we are naturally affluent because the Source Supreme supports every need and desire. We lack nothing, because our essential nature is one of purity with the Source Supreme.

## Self-Contemplation on Divine Love

State to your Self: Today, *Now,* I will apply the Law of Giving and Divine Love. I put it into effect by making a commitment to silently send Divine Love to whomever I meet or encounter.

Divine Love and Giving are one: *Remember, the more you give the more you get in all aspects of your life.*

Now go to your place where you will not be disturbed, sit erect in your chair, and read the following statement 3 times. When completed close your eyes, open your heart and contemplate upon these beautiful words:

*Divine love must be demonstrated not spoken. It requires a positive attitude, focused attention, and action to fill your heart with ITS essence. Your eternal survival and happiness will be realized through the understanding and conscious cooperation with the Divine Law. Spiritual growth demands that you exert the highest degree of Divine Love from Soul. Divine Love imparts vitality to your heart and mind and enables it to germinate through you and throughout the Universes of Source Supreme. The law of Divine Love will bring to you all necessity for your spiritual growth and maturity. If you desire to be loved, the only way to receive love is by giving love. The more you give, the more you get. You must open your heart and fill your Self with Divine Love, until you become a magnet of Divine Love.*

Be still, see *your* Light and hear *your* Sound.

# CHAPTER 10

## THE INNER TEMPLE

As an awakened Soul, you have already visited the Inner Temple often, sometimes with your dream body and sometimes as Soul, with conscious awareness.

In Chapter 5 we introduced a chart of the Heavenly Realms. If you have been practicing the Self-Contemplations you may now be more familiar with these Subtle Realms and understand their significance to you as Soul.

Each of these Realms has a Spiritual Guardian and special teaching on how to live as a spiritual vehicle for Source Supreme. These Spiritual Guardians work directly with Source Supreme for the liberation of Souls.

In the Realms below the Soul Plane, matter is extremely dense. These are the Realms where false teachers work to trap Souls. These false ones will say they are guiding you to the truth, so beware. They will say they want you to listen to your inner guidance, but this is a distortion because they really want you to listen to their directives.

This is important, because what is referred to as the Inner Temple by the false ones is not the true Inner Temple.

What is this Inner Temple we speak of and what is its importance? The Inner Temple is the gateway to connecting with the Light and Sound in the Highest Heavenly Realm where Source Supreme resides. You can experience for yourself the Heavenly Realms by practicing the Self-Contemplations given in this book.

As you practice with discernment, discipline and Divine Love, you can directly access the invisible worlds of Source Supreme. By practicing these spiritual exercises you access the Inner Temple with *direct connection and communication* with Source Supreme.

Whatever you need to know, whatever guidance you seek is available to you without any intermediary by entering into that silence at the Inner Temple. This is a powerful experience leading you to know who and what you are, where you came from, where you are going and the qualities of Omnipotence, Omniscience and Omnipresence.

Here is where you directly access Truth in its purest form. Here is where you are renewed and refreshed by communing with the Light and Sound also known as the Spiritual Nectar or Jivan Mukti. Here is where the wisdom of the Heavenly worlds is available to you and you can commune directly with IT.

A true Spiritual Master will tell you it is not necessary to take anyone's word, or to blindly believe. The True Master will tell you to "Go Within" and check for yourself what is true. This means to sit in silence, go to your Inner Temple and KNOW firsthand.

Since both the true Spiritual Master, and the false ones have now given this instruction this presents a challenge for you. If a false teacher directs you to go within to find answers it requires great awareness to remain discerning. One way to recognize the lies is to listen for jargon and insistence that you are "special" and "chosen." This is to appeal to *vanity.*

When you practice the Self-Contemplations always ask to be shown the truth about any teacher by their vibrations, not by their title or the number of their followers.

By going within and becoming consciously aware of the sounds in each of the Heavenly Realms, you protect yourself from believing that the visions and experiences in the Astral Realm are the highest truth. What is learned on the Astral, Causal and Mental Realms has limited value to you in full awakening.

Do you need a Spiritual Master? Yes and No. It is better to proceed on your own with the Self-Contemplations than to follow a teacher who can only take you to the Astral or Mental Realms. A true Spiritual Master also bestows *Initiation* on you, Soul, and your spiritual radiance and power increases with each

Initiation. Initiation is essential for full liberation and awakening.

However, if you are ready, no one or thing can stop you from physically meeting the authentic Spiritual Master of the Time. The Initiation into the Sound Current of Life does not have to be formal with a ritual or a ceremony. You could be out shopping, at work or play, and the sacred meeting between you and the Spiritual Master Teacher could be a passing glance, direct eye contact or a simple knowingness that a stranger, the Spiritual Master has recognized you are ready and "hooked you up" and fine-tuned the Sound Current within you, Soul, so you can proceed into the pure Higher Heavenly Worlds. At times, one of His authorized Spiritually Advanced Initiates may also give you a silent Initiation.

Kabir was a well known saint and spiritual master who warned that in this Kali Yuga, there will be twelve false masters working to lure you and keep you from the One True Master.

In full awakening you and the Spiritual Master are united, so you are the Inner Master. With consistent and dedicated practice we realize there is no separation between Source Supreme and Soul... That YOU ARE The Inner Master.

Then every breath we take, every word we speak, every thought we think and every action can be a reflection of this conscious knowing. We become a vehicle for the expression of the Divine Spirit.

When we know truth rather than believe what comes from outside and because we have consistently visited the Inner Temple and relied on the wisdom we gather there via our divine connection with Source Supreme, we find we have a new inner confidence and serenity.

In this way, fear and doubt are eliminated. We have a new security. A real and lasting security. A security that is not dependent on anything exterior. It is an interior, inner knowingness that gives us great peace. We no longer rely on the words of an outside source whether it is a government, a corporation, a group, an individual or any entity other than ourselves and we become Free.

Freedom from control or fear directed at us from outside sources loses its power when we are in alignment with Source Supreme and rely on our own connection by going to the Inner Temple.

The Inner Temple is best accessed by strengthening our connection with the Light and Sound of Source Supreme. Chanting or singing the sacred names of Source Supreme often precedes preparation for initiation into the Highest Heavenly Realms.

HU is the sacred celestial Original Sound Current or "Word" of Source Supreme. The HU is chanted or sung as the name of God. It can also be used to refer to the ethereal Sound Current known as the Music of the Spheres, Planes or Heavens.

Sometimes pronounced "HOO" or "HUUU" it symbolizes, and even mimics, the Original Sound Current, and is used in a special way to refer to the Nameless God, the One Whose Real Name is unpronounceable, truly beyond all earthly languages.

The Supreme Being or Source Supreme has been called by various names in different languages, but the mystics, saints and true spiritual masters have known IT as HU, the natural name, not-man-made, the only name of the Nameless, which all nature constantly proclaims.

"Hoo" or "HU" is a very beautiful and soothing name of God, the Source Supreme. It can be pronounced as: HUGH or HOO. It is truly a love-song to God, the Beloved Lord of All.

An Eastern Sufi Spiritual Master, Sultan Bahu, once said, "There are few genuine disciples. People purporting to be masters perpetuate themselves with false promises. They exploit their followers to satisfy their greed." Bahu also warned everyone to watch out for false teachers who want to be masters over others even though they have never been faithful and loyal disciples themselves.

"These false prophets were never disciples themselves. Rather, they contrive to make disciples of others as an act of seeming charity. Instead, they swindle their disciples of their money and belongings."

"If a master does not end your pain of separation, he is not even worth calling a Master. Who would even need the kind of master who does not bestow spiritual blessing? Why even go to the kind of teacher who is incapable of giving proper instruction?"

Unfortunately there are several Eastern and Western groups, acting under the guise of religious and spiritual organizations, that have misused the sacred name of Source Supreme, the HU, with their students or practitioners. These groups are actually cults. Please beware. *You do not have to join anything or go anywhere to commune with Source Supreme. All ground is Holy.*

On this genuine path of the lover of Divine Spirit and the Beloved God, there is no need for plagiarizing texts, becoming a fake guru, falsifying one's past history or resume. Spirituality cannot be photocopied or photo shopped. It must be lived, experienced. One enjoys the connection with others on an established spiritual path, being part of a community as a humble student, having an overflowing gratitude for the association with a living spiritual Master, a connection to be forever celebrated.

If you wish to learn the art of dying daily while awakening and living in the Spiritual world of Source Supreme, learn to go directly. Sit in silent reverence of Source Supreme and follow the HU.

The Self-Contemplations in this book will gently guide you to the Original Source of All, without a social community and the social interaction and reinforcements of potluck dinners and campouts. The true spiritual path is within YOU, and only YOU can achieve the Higher Spiritual Worlds on your own by making the conscious effort.

## Awaken in the Heavenly Worlds

**The Blue Star, Divine Love,
You, Soul, The Inner Master**

# ADVANCED SPIRITUAL SELF-CONTEMPLATIONS OPERATING IN AND FROM THE HEAVENLY WORLDS

## *Advanced Spiritual Protection Self-Contemplation*

In Chapter One, you started your Spiritual Awakening with a Spiritual Protection Self-Contemplation. As you advance and awaken into the Higher Heavenly Worlds, you, Soul, will be further away from your bodies. That is, your *attention* will be removed from your dense bodies, as you explore your true home of Source Supreme. It is vital that you protect these dense and subtle bodies while on your Spiritual Awakenings. The following enhanced Self-Contemplation will fortify your original White Light Protection Technique.

You are going to strengthen your energy field and erect a stronger spiritual barrier that will be impossible for any negativity to penetrate or overcome.

Retreat to your quiet place, sit erect and become relaxed and comfortable. Close your eyes and breathe very deeply until you can sense any tensions easing and your attention turning to your world within.

As with your original Spiritual Protective Technique, see the powerful luminous White Light entering the top of your head flowing downward to your Heart and Solar Plexus area, then expanding like the rays of the Sun filling your entire body. Every cell and atom in your body glows with ITS essence. Feel the substance, the power and the warmth. See it flowing out of your hands, feet and entire body. You *become* the pure White Light.

Start breathing in and out more deeply, and notice your radiant White Light aura expanding as you breathe in, and contracting as you breathe out. Continue to breathe in and out until you realize that your protective shield has expanded into an egg-shaped balloon with you in the center. Remember there are no limitations such as ceilings, walls, floors, etc. Your radiant egg shield has no boundaries.

As you continue to breathe in and out, and your protective egg expands, it no longer contracts but continues to inflate like a balloon. Notice how hard your protective egg shield has become. Realize that no negativity can penetrate your shield. Only positive energy and Divine Love can enter.

You are now going to take your White Light Shield a step further, doubling your protection by adding extremely sharp spikes that are like hardened nails. These spikes of White Light will emerge from your protective egg extending outwardly in all directions. You can think of it like the defensive quills of a porcupine preparing to defend itself. Any negativity that may come your way will be immediately dissolved if any of your shining sharp spikes of light are touched.

Make sure your new Spiritual defenses are always wrapped tightly around your Physical body. Know that you can make these defenses any size you need them to be. Practice this technique at least every other day until it becomes natural, so that you can call upon this extra defense any time and anywhere you may need it.

*Remember, this Spiritual protection is used in conjunction with your regular journeys into the Heavenly Worlds.*

## Self-Contemplation for the Dream State

A valuable step on your journey is to recognize the benefit that the dream state holds for your spiritual evolution. Your dreams can reveal what is in the subconscious mind, including the bothersome karmic patterns in your life. Eventually your dreams become more clear and luminous. In the dream state it is possible to help crush the seeds of future karma from ripening. This means that you become more conscious in your dream state and become cause instead of effect and can choose spiritually positive behaviors even in your dreams. This is also where you can meet with an authentic Spiritual Teacher and be given instructions on how to progress with your spiritual journey.

There are many spiritual practices for advancing spiritually during dreamtime. You can also practice awakening the power of your imagination during the dream state. One technique to accomplish this is given here:

While lying in bed, just before going to sleep, listen for the life giving Sound Current vibrating in the middle of your head (the pineal gland area.) Now, imagine your Crown Chakra opening like the soft petals of a beautiful, fragrant rose, a lily or a lotus flower. Feel each petal 'click' open, as your entire head becomes this magnificent flower. The petals open fully, one by one, as the enchanting music of the spheres, the Sound Current pulls you, Soul, gently upward toward the Divine Light. The Light is brighter than a million Suns, warm and powerful. The aroma of this beautiful flower becomes more fragrant as Soul leaves the Physical Realm.

As you pass through the various Realms of the inner dimensions, a radiant Spiritual Being greets you. You may challenge this Being with the sentence "In the name of Source Supreme show yourself." A true Spiritual Friend or Master will stay with you, otherwise they will dissipate. The possibilities of what you may experience in the Heavenly Realms during dream time is both real and unlimited.

Since most of us spend 5 to 8 hours each night in the dream state, it is important that your dream state reflects your spiritual progress.

## *Advanced Self-Healing Contemplation*

You begin your Higher Journey with a Self-Healing technique. This may be familiar to you if you have been searching for the Higher Spiritual knowledge. We include this technique because it works.

Allow yourself at least a half hour. Go to your quiet place and once again sit erect, feet flat on the floor, hands in your lap. Be comfortable, loosen your clothes, and then take many deep breaths. Close your eyes and place your head down so your chin touches the bottom of your neck meeting your chest.

See and feel with your Spiritual eyes the luminous White Light of Source Supreme enter your Crown Chakra flowing through the top of your head. IT is so bright and pure that IT is a translucent mist filling your entire physical body. Notice how warm, relaxed and calm you feel as it enters your heart and solar plexus. You are at peace with all life. Any pains, anxieties, nervousness and ailments are beginning to dissolve as this luminous White Mist flows through your body.

Start by placing your attention on your left foot. See the White Light filling your toes, gradually rising up as it flows into and fills your ankle and the calf of your left leg. Feel its soothing power as it is gently pulling upward. Know that it is cleansing and healing that entire area as it clears blockages in your muscles, veins, arteries, and blood vessels.

Now move your attention to your right foot and do the exact same thing as you did with the left side of your Physical body.

Once this is completed go back to your left side and see the White Current of Source Supreme rise up through your knee, your left thigh and genital region wrapping around your front and back like a beautiful luminous belt of healing purity. Know that it is also penetrating and healing your kidneys and other vital physical organs. Deep cleaning ever so gently as it continues to pull you upward toward your Crown Chakra.

Now do the same with your right side starting with the knee area. The entire lower half of your physical body should be translucent.

Begin again and see the white light go up and through your stomach, chest, around your back healing all your organs; your liver, kidneys, pancreas, lungs, heart, etc. Feel the Divine Current pulling upward through your spinal column to your neck. The White Light Current is much stronger now. It is so strong that it is pulling your tucked down neck and head erect.

The White Light is now flowing upward and healing your neck, mouth, nose, teeth, eyes, and hair. The holy Current flows and pulsates out the top of your head, your Crown Chakra.

This purifying translucent mist of White Light is flowing as a beautiful fountain exploding in the air from the top of your head, falling down and sparkling all around you. The Sound Current of life is so powerful that it is pulling you upward in a most pleasurable, soothing experience.

Stay in this uplifting state as long as possible. Really enjoy it. Know that all your ailments have been erased in the Current of Source Supreme. When ready awaken gently, renewed, refreshed and healed.

## Soul Plane Experience Self-Contemplation

Sat Nam is the spiritual guardian and true teacher of the Fifth Plane above the Lower Worlds. To have this blissful experience, once again go to your place of peace, sit erect, close your eyes and take some very deep breaths. Release the tensions of the day and calm yourself. Still your mind.

Before singing the 'Word Name' of this glorious Higher Dimension and Being, *ask Divine Spirit, in all humbleness, to meet with Sat Nam and to be given and taught a specific lesson just for you.*

If you are fortunate to meet this great Golden Being and receive His wisdom, just be still and absorb what may be given to you. Communication is not what you think...no words will be spoken. Information will be transferred *Soul to Soul and you will just know.*

Gently begin to sing or chant His name SAT NAM – "SAT-NAAA-MMMMMM." Hold the "M" and stretch it out a little longer. Sing this holy name 6-12 times, then let go and pay attention. It will take you directly to the Soul Plane.

If you are fortunate the first time attempting this contemplation, and you have earned the right, you may find yourself in a beautiful golden temple filled with *brilliant golden light* sitting and listening to the wisdom of Sat Nam. The information and wisdom that He gives you *is only for you.* It is for you to free yourself from the negative bonds of the Lower Worlds. Be extremely grateful. If you do not succeed the first time in meeting with Sat Nam, continue this exercise daily *until you realize that you have awakened to this reality.* You may even have an encounter with Sat Nam in the Dream state.

You may find yourself visiting with Sat Nam on many occasions before reaching into Higher Heavenly Worlds. You will know when you are ready to advance.

## The God Realms Self-Contemplation: Source Supreme

When you feel you are ready, take your quiet position, choose and sing any one of the following blessed words of the Higher Worlds 6-12 times and relax and learn.

*SHANTI – "Shan-Teeeeee".*

*HUM – "Huuuummmm".*

*Aluk – Aaaa-LuuuuK" snap the "Kha" at the end.*

*HUK – HuuuuuK" snap the "Kha" at the end.*

If you feel comfortable and/or are having success with the vibration of a particular "word" and Dimension, stay with it for a while and learn all you can.

## The HU: Source Supreme Self-Contemplation

Take your comfortable position; keep your attention on the inner window of your temple, your Spiritual Eye. Then place your Self, Soul, 3-5 feet behind your head. Begin to sing the HU in a long drawn out manner 6-12 times. "Huuuuuuuuu"

You are bringing the Divine Sound Current, the HU, into your Physical Being. When the Current is strong, pay attention and catch the rhythm of the returning wavelength of this Current. It will gently pull you upward in Soul and out through your Crown Chakra moving you directly into the Realm of Source Supreme.

## A Gentle Reflection

Soul can be in any one of three places:

1   Lodged in the physical body, either in the heart
    area or the head.

2   Some Souls can actually run a physical body
    about 5-10 feet from the unit.

3   Advanced Souls can maintain and operate a
    physical body miles away.

Do not place limitations upon your Self. Cast off all doubt and fear and break free of the prison of lies and ignorance. There are many uncharted Dimensions to explore. Possibly one day you may serve and assist in the running of the worlds of Source Supreme.

You are only limited by the lack of an awakened imagination. When you fully awaken and realize who and what you are, as Soul, you will find there is no need for the faculty of imagination any longer. Just Be.

When you can call up any image and manifest at will, you become the master, the master of your fate.

You are and have always been spiritually free. You are a King or Queen of nobility. Claim your God-given right of spiritual Self-mastership Here and Now. Awaken to the Majesty of Source Supreme.

*Continued Blessings in Divine Love.*